1927

P⁴ 4 R C Trevelyan

TO

JOHN BAILEY

ENGLISH SONGS
OF ITALIAN FREEDOM

CHOSEN AND ARRANGED

WITH AN INTRODUCTION BY

GEORGE MACAULAY TREVELYAN

LONGMANS, GREEN, AND CO.
39 PATERNOSTER ROW, LONDON
NEW YORK, BOMBAY, AND CALCUTTA
1911

I RENDER my best acknowledgments and thanks for permission to use copyright: to Mr. Watts Dunton in the case of the poems of Swinburne; to Messrs. Constable and Company, Limited, London, and Messrs. Charles Scribner's Sons, New York, in the case of Meredith; to Mrs. Hamilton King in the case of her sonnet on *Garibaldi*, and to her publishers, Messrs. Kegan Paul, Trench and Co., in the case of the extract from *The Disciples*.

'It is no great matter, supposing that Italy could be liberated, who or what is sacrificed. It is a grand object —the very *poetry* of politics. Only think—a free Italy!!'

Feb. 18, 1821.   BYRON.

'As the sunrise to the night,
    As the north wind to the clouds,
  As the earthquake's fiery flight
    Ruining mountain solitudes;
  Everlasting Italy,
  Be those hopes and fears on thee.'
                                        SHELLEY.

INTRODUCTION

THE influence of poetry upon English life is smaller to-day than it was during the first eighty years of the nineteenth century. So little is poetry held in account by those who set the tone of thought and feeling to our generation, that when the Victorian age is condemned as narrow, parochial, and petty, it is scarcely held to be a plea in mitigation that it was the age of the Brownings and Tennyson, of Swinburne and Matthew Arnold, of Macaulay as a ballad-writer, of William Morris and Rossetti, of Carlyle and of Meredith. Nearly all these poets acquired the commanding influence only attained by writers characteristic of the epoch in which they live. It was not a mere accident that the public whom they inspired and represented was drawn during the 'fifties and 'sixties into a national enthusiasm for the cause of Italian freedom, a movement of political opinion as closely connected with literature and poetry as the anti-slavery movement of the previous generation had been connected with evangelical religion. Each of these movements left a deep mark on our social and intellectual life, though each came to a sudden termination on the complete success of the causes advocated, the one in 1833 with the liberation of the slaves, the other in 1870 with the final completion of the Italian kingdom.

Like the greater struggle for the abolition of slavery in the British Empire, the English movement in aid of Italian freedom stood a little outside the ordinary lines of party controversy. It deserves the notice of posterity, not so much on account of its importance as a factor in the liberation of Italy—though that was by no means negligible—but because it was England's most characteristic attitude in the mid-nineteenth century, and the 'breath of finer air' to our countrymen during a few years otherwise somewhat torpid in their Palmerstonian self-complacency.

We are too near our own time to compare ourselves judicially with our fathers and grandfathers. But some differences may be noted, without prejudice to either generation. The men who had been nurtured on ancient and modern poetry, and on an ethical and idealist view of history, saw the most interesting event of their time in the renaissance of Italian freedom. They thought it natural that England should lend a hand, or at least a voice, to the right side in that contest. Whereas their descendants, who divide their literary allegiance between Mr. Kipling on the one hand, and Mr. Shaw and the novelists of social change on the other, have banished from their outlook on foreign affairs all virtues and vices but those which are strictly self-regarding, and have taken with unparalleled eagerness to questions concerning the daily life of men and women in our own island.

The Victorian mind is indeed already so remote

INTRODUCTION

from all the conflicting influences of our own age, that a study of some characteristic piece of Victorian idealism might be suggestive of much. But it is with no such historical or philosophic motive, but in devotion to the Muse of Poetry, that I have beguiled some heavy hours by gathering together these *English Songs of Italian Freedom*. I feel no anxiety about the reception of this little book, for the failure to please others with that which was done to please myself will not disappoint me. The fruits of an idle summer month can only attract fellow-idlers, and idlers, having time to think, are of all mankind the most critical. But if any one is found to approve, it will be on the ground that the placing together of poems inspired by a common theme may, in some sort, reproduce the atmosphere in which they were composed, and so enhance the effect of each ; and that a slight service is rendered to lovers of poetry not acquainted with the details of Italian history, by the Introduction and notes in this volume. Swinburne's magnificent *Halt before Rome*, the last uproarious stanzas of Browning's *Old Pictures in Florence*, and many of his wife's best poems, referred to events and persons familiar to all half a century ago, but now very dimly remembered. In such cases I have held that explanations should be adjusted liberally to the needs of the least learned. And if, for every two readers who are annoyed at being told in the notes what they knew before, there is one who is grateful for being ' edified by the margent,' I shall be well content.

ENGLISH SONGS OF ITALIAN FREEDOM

The decline of Italy from the leadership of Europe in arts, literature, learning, and commerce took place during the hundred years of the Reformation and Counter - Reformation, while Luther, Calvin, and Loyola were transforming the world. The century of so much progress and liberation to northern Europe was the dark era for Italy, when her sons forfeited the national independence which they had maintained, in spite of their divisions, throughout the whole of the Middle Ages. In the sixteenth century the Peninsula was conquered by French, Germans, and Spaniards, and of these various foreign dominations who struggled together for the prize, the worst emerged victor. The barbarous and bigoted Spaniards, bringing with them their Jesuits and their Inquisition, made the Pope the servant of their fanaticism and their lust of cruelty, and turned the countrymen of Dante, Savonarola and Michael Angelo into a race of slaves and hypocrites. Learning and thought were suppressed, and art withered, flourishing last in Venice because there the Pope, the Spaniard, and the Inquisition were long kept at arm's length. In Shakespeare's day, while the memory of free Italian culture was transmuting our own literature into something rich and strange, Italy herself died and was buried, and the ghoulish shapes of the priest, the inquisitor, and the Spanish spearman sat upon the grave of all that had once been fair.

For two hundred years there was no resurrection. About the middle decade of this dreary epoch, Italy changed masters. The Spanish rule, grown by its

own abominable vices too effete even to maintain its
hold upon dead Italy, yielded the prey to the Austrian,
as a consequence of the victories of Marlborough and
Eugène. Austrian influence dominated in the Peninsula throughout the eighteenth century. If there
had been anything good left to destroy, the new-
comers might not have been so active in destruction
as the Spaniard had formerly proved himself, but the
Austrian drill sergeant was only too efficient in main-
taining the system of blank negation that he inherited
from the last of the Spaniards.

The first awakening of Italy came from without,
from across the French Alps. The first epoch of the
Risorgimento ('resurrection,' as the Italians call it) is
the Napoleonic occupation from 1796 to 1814. On
this account alone the debt of Italy to France is
immeasurable. But it is a gratifying and romantic
circumstance that the ideas and armies of the French
Revolution came into Italy under the leadership of a
man of Italian origin, a 'prince' of the spiritual stock
of Macchiavelli and the Borgias. Napoleon, not very
tenderly, but most effectually, raised his mother
Italy, still but half-conscious, out of the death-trance
of two centuries. For half a generation he gave her
rational and modern government. The old petty
despotisms were swept away, and the greater part of
the Peninsula was governed as if it were a nation,
subject, indeed, to the Napoleonic French Empire,
but as the Italian province thereof. The *Code
Napoléon* instead of mediæval laws ; efficient bureau-
cracy instead of the arbitrary whims of decadent

tyrants by right divine ; modern education on scientific and military lines instead of clerical obscurantism ; the encouragement of the professional and middle classes on the principle of *carrière ouverte aux talents*, instead of caste privilege,—such was the Napoleonic system by which Italians were educated to become capable in the next generation of rebellion on their own behalf, and ultimately of self-government.

The first advent of the young Napoleon into Italy was hailed by Ugo Foscolo, the first poet of the actual *Risorgimento*, as the advent of Liberty herself :—

> ' Ma tu dell' Alpi dall' äerie cime
> Al rintronar di trombe e di timballi
> Ausonia guati e giù piombi col volo,
>
> . . . . .
>
> Gallia intuona e diffonde
> Di Libertade il nome
> E mare e cielo Libertà risponde.' [1]

Foscolo's poems are titanic and grandiose, suited to their age and subject. They reflect the appalling chiaroscuro of the French Revolutionary and Napoleonic epochs — when the light of new, vast hopes for the rapid perfecting of the human race and the return of the golden age played on the surface of Cimmerian darkness and, if they did not cure, at least revealed the horror of the world's old cruelty and law of force. ' Shadows of prophecy shiver along by the lakes and the rivers and mutter across the ocean.'

Leipsic restored the *ancien régime* in Italy, and

[1] *Bonaparte Liberatore, Oda del liber' uomo Niccolò Ugo Foscolo,* 1797, prima del 12 maggio.

xii

INTRODUCTION

Waterloo ensured it for a generation to come. In 1816 Ugo Foscolo sought refuge in England, the first in that long roll of honour—of the Italian exiles in our country. The Austrian bore rule in the north of the Peninsula, the Pope in the centre, and elsewhere the petty despots whose authority rested henceforth on the moral influence of the confessional and the physical fact of the Austrian bayonets. Napoleon, the profligate of all men's blood and money, was little regretted even in Italy at the first moment of his fall. But in a few years, almost in a few months, the educated part of the community felt the heavy difference. After the Napoleonic interlude, the *ancien régime* was intolerable to the laity, to the middle classes, to the working men of the towns. The Austrians, less *simpatici* than the French, were hateful to all classes of natives, even to the more conservative nobles and peasantry. The first fifteen years after Waterloo, before Mazzini had fused the national discontent into a positive purpose with an aim ahead, were years of mere anger and despair. One great Italian and two great English poets have immortalised this dark moment in Italian history.

Leopardi, the contemporary of Shelley and Byron, is the poet of despair, as befitted a subject of the Pope in that dreadful epoch between Napoleon's fall and Mazzini's rise.

> ' Ahi troppo tardi
> E nella sera dell' umane cose
> Acquista oggi chi nasce il moto e il senso.'

> ' Alas ! too late,
> And in the evening tide of human things
> The child who 's born to-day must move and feel.'

In that despair, utterly irremediable as it was for Leopardi's own soul, how much hope lay for Italy! Far sadder would it have been if Leopardi, instead of despairing, had shrugged his shoulders, and taught the noblest spirits of his time and country mockingly to accept the rule of priests and foreigners as a thing inevitable, and therefore at all endurable. If Italy had still been content in the nineteenth century with the conditions which she had endured in the eighteenth, then both she and Leopardi might have been happy as penned sheep are happy. Despair like that of Leopardi, which had never been felt in the easy-going eighteenth century, was a measure of the work that Napoleon had done for Italy. He had saved her from being ever again content under the *mali governi*. Leopardi, in addressing his sister on the occasion of her marriage in 1821, used these terrible words :—

> 'O miseri, o codardi
> Figliuoli avrai, miseri eleggi.'

'O my sister, thou must needs bear children to be either unhappy or cowardly; choose then the unhappy.'

That epigram sums up the spirit of the Italian martyrdom of the generation that followed. The blank choice between misery and cowardice was nobly made by many Italians in every corner of the land.

There is a difference between the pessimism of Leopardi and the pessimism of some others. For his despair is not that of a man posing to the public, or denying virtue that he may enjoy vice, but of a man most terribly in earnest. It is significant that

INTRODUCTION

Mr. Gladstone, at once the most optimistic and the most Christian of statesmen, should have felt for Leopardi, the denier, an admiration which he would never have extended to a spirit that had not some kinship with his own. No doubt he recognised that Leopardi's contempt for the life of man as he saw it lived in the territories of the Pope was not the pessimism that discourages from action and from virtue, but the cry of rage that may awaken the souls of the sleepers. And so indeed it proved.

Leopardi, looking on the ruins of past greatness with which Italy is covered, wrote the famous lines to which Swinburne has referred in his *Siena* [1] :—

> 'O patria mia, vedo le mura e gli archi
> E le colonne e i simulacri e l'erme
> Torri degli avi nostri
> Ma la gloria non vedo.'

'O my country, I see the walls and the arches and the columns and the statues and the lonely towers of our forefathers, but the glory I do not see.'

Where indeed was the glory? But since then a light of glory has arisen and passed over the ruins of ancient Italy, the glory of her ' resurrection,' a tale which will for ever remain among the most inspiring of the true legends of the human race.

[1]
> 'The weary poet, thy sad son,
> Upon thy soil, under thy skies,
> Saw all Italian things save one—
> Italia; this thing missed his eyes;
> The old mother-night, the breast, the face,
> That reared, that lit the Roman race;
> This not Leopardi saw . . .'

During the years of Leopardi's lonely pain, Italy harboured two strangers who, like him, mourned over the ruins not only of Italian art and greatness, but of Italian liberty. Shelley and Byron began the English song-book of the *Risorgimento*. The most musical dirge over dead liberty is Shelley's *Lines written among the Euganean Hills* (in October 1818), with the prospect at his feet of Venice and of the Lombard plain enclosed by Alps, Apennines, and sea, still enslaved ' under the mighty Austrian.' There is little of hope in this poem. But when, two years later, the Carbonari of Naples rose in arms and forced a constitution on their Bourbon king, the hopes of all Italy, and of Shelley and Byron, suddenly rose high. Shelley wrote the *Ode to Naples* in honour of the awakening of Italian liberty. But it was only the first sickly stirring of the sleeper, and the watchers by the bedside were no friends to the patient. The Austrian armies, who seemed to Shelley's imagination

> ' Earth-born Forms
> Arrayed against the ever-living gods,'

marched down by order of the Holy Alliance through the length of Italy, suppressed the Neapolitan constitution, and conducted just such another cruel and bloody execution upon the best men of the professional and educated classes as had been conducted under Nelson's ægis more than twenty years before. But on this occasion England stood apart as neutral. The day was coming when she would be on the right side, and that day was prepared by the zeal with which

Byron took up the Italian cause. For, in spite of the outcries of his respectable fellow-countrymen against him, the outcast sinner exerted over them ' an influence more than episcopal.'

Byron discovered and assimilated into his own life the best as well as the worst that was doing in his land of exile. If intimacy with Italians proved his bane in Venice, it was his soul's salvation next year at Ravenna. He joined himself to the *carbonari*, the vigorous and warlike peasants and gentlemen of the Romagna—the fathers of the men who saved Garibaldi in 1849—who were themselves, as early as 1821, conspiring to throw off the degrading yoke of the Papal Government. Byron made practical preparations to fight, and if necessary to die, with his Italian friends, in case, as he most earnestly hoped, the rebellion at Naples should spread to the Romagna. Nothing but the too easy suppression of the South by the Austrian troops sent him to die for Greece instead of for Italy.

' To-day,' he writes on February 18, 1821, ' I have had no communication with my Carbonari cronies ; but in the mean time my lower apartments are full of their bayonets, fusils, cartridges, and what not. I suppose that they consider me as a depôt, to be sacrificed, in case of accidents. It is no great matter, supposing that Italy could be liberated, who or what is sacrificed. It is a grand object—the very *poetry* of politics. Only think—a free Italy ! ! ! '

A few days later he writes that all is at an end. ' The plan has missed—the chiefs are betrayed, military as well as civil. . . . I always had an idea that it would be bungled ; but was willing to hope, and am so still. Whatever I can do by money, means, or person, I will venture freely for their freedom ; and have so repeated to them (some of their chiefs) half an hour ago. I have 2500 scudi, better than 500 pounds, in the house, which I offered to begin with.' *

Here was the splendid side of Byron, which more than redeems so much egoism, foppery, and vice. He was the first Englishman who saw, in those dark days, that the Italians had a cause and a purpose of their own. Divesting himself of his English prejudices in their company, he lent these poor people his powerful aid, and was only too willing to give them a life which others of his countrymen, had they possessed his wealth, fame, and genius, would certainly have valued more highly than to make a present of it to Romagnole peasants or Greek bandits. The new fact that a living Italy was struggling beneath the outward semblance of Metternich's 'order' was thus perceived by Byron, first of Englishmen, and by the 'pard-like Spirit, beautiful and swift,' who moved at his side through the Italian cities.

The era of the early Carbonaro risings—of Leopardi, Byron, and Shelley—was followed by the era of Mazzini's 'Young Italy' propaganda from 1831 to 1848. In the 'Manifesto of Young Italy,' issued by Mazzini in 1831, we read that Italy must be founded

* Byron's *Works*, Murray, 1901. *Letters and Journals*, vol. v., a volume that gives the best of Byron.

other writer, whether historian or poet, has merely
played with the subject of Mazzini's personality.*

From 1837 until his death in 1872 he resided princi-
pally in our island, making numerous and intimate
friends. ' Italy is my country,' he said, ' but England
is my real home, if I have any.' Before the end he had
grown actually to love the fogs and the hazy London
atmosphere, in which the prophet seems to have found
the sorrows and shortcomings of mankind more
softened and bearable than amid the hard, clear
outlines revealed beneath the Italian sky.

The year 1848, which saw the whole of continental
Europe ablaze with revolution, was the year of Italy's
great struggle to liberate herself without aid from
France or any other country. The watchword of the
year was *Italia farà da se*, ' Italy shall do it for herself.'
By a mighty effort of enthusiasm she achieved her
freedom for a few weeks, thrusting back the Austrian
armies out of Lombardy and Venice into the fortresses
of the Quadrilateral. Meanwhile, Sicily had thrown
off the yoke of the Bourbons, and the inhabitants of
Naples, of Rome, of Tuscany, and of Piedmont secured
constitutions from their native rulers, of whom only
one kept faith when the danger was past. The
spring of 1848 was the ideal moment of the Italian
risorgimento, a more perfect theme for poets than
even those grand events which finally secured her

* In saying this I do not mean to detract from the merits of
Mr. Bolton King's *Life of Mazzini*, and the remarks on Mazzini in
Mr. Herbert Fisher's *Republican Tradition in Europe*.

freedom a dozen years later. But the division of classes, provinces, and parties, the want of steady purpose in Naples and Tuscany, the want of such a man as Cavour at the helm of Piedmont, led to the reconquest of North Italy by the white-haired Austrian Field-Marshal Radetzky in the late summer of 1848, and to the fall of the revolutionary governments in the Centre and South. For twelve months the movement gradually crumbled in town after town, and province after province, of the Peninsula. The end came in the summer of 1849, with the heroic defence of Mazzini's short-lived Roman republic against the French armies, by the northern volunteers under Garibaldi, and the no less heroic defence of Venice against the Austrians by its own citizens under Manin.

The drama of this great Italian effort of 1848-49 has rightly received more attention in English literature than any other phase of the Italian *risorgimento*. Our poets and our great poetical novelist have not merely sung its praises, but have analysed and criticised its strength and weakness with insight such as the writers of one country seldom have shown for the affairs of another. Some knowledge of the Italian character and of *Risorgimento* history enables the reader of Meredith's *Vittoria* to perceive that it is not only a great prose poem on an epic moment in human affairs, but a detailed and accurate analysis of a people and of a period. Most historical novels are composed, at second hand, out of history books, but *Vittoria* sprang fully armed from Meredith's living knowledge of the primary authorities—Italian patriots and time, were more interested in Rome, and less in Greece ; Virgil and Cicero were still in vogue ; the Vatican sculptures and Pompeii were the goal of such as would now pass on to the Parthenon and to Delphi, to Crete or to Egypt. If foreign travel was less common than to-day, it was more concentrated upon Italy, and the charm of her landscapes and cities became associated in sympathetic English minds with the cause of the inhabitants of the country. Indeed, it was impossible to visit the Peninsula without seeing clear signs of an odious oppression. Meanwhile, in England many of the best Italians of a great Italian era were congregated in exile, living on terms of close social intercourse with our chief political and literary families. Mazzini, Panizzi, Saffi, Poerio, Lacaita, and many others enjoyed the personal affections of their English hosts as no other body of refugees ever did before or since. The important and startling conversion of Mr. Gladstone to the Italian cause in 1851, no less than the warm attachment to that cause of Lord John Russell, of the Brownings, and of Tennyson, can be clearly traced to these conditions of literature and scholarship, of society and travel.

If such were the intellectual affinities binding England to Italy, there was also at that period a very general and ardent theoretic belief in the virtues of free government, such as had not existed in England fifty years earlier, and does not exist so strongly to-day among the upper and middle classes. In the 'fifties and 'sixties Mill was the leading philosopher, Hampden, Sydney, and Washington were regarded as national heroes, Macaulay and Motley were universally read, and history was conceived as essentially the history of liberty. The propertied classes in England, having recently established their power by revolt against a narrow oligarchy in 1832, and not yet feeling that power seriously threatened by the still unenfranchised working class, were disposed to regard despotism with abhorrence, and parliamentary government with enthusiasm.

British sentiment in favour of Italian liberty, favoured by these general causes, was further enhanced when the patriotic movement in Italy ceased to be Republican and became associated with the parliamentary monarchy of Victor Emmanuel of Piedmont, so ably developed by Cavour in acknowledged imitation of the English system. The tide of sympathy for the Italian cause ran high, when in 1859 a cross-current for a few months distracted and bewildered British opinion. Napoleon III. undertook to liberate North Italy from Austria, and marched his armies into the Lombard plain, in alliance with Victor Emmanuel's Piedmontese. Now our fathers had one sentiment as strong as their sympathy with Italy, and that was their fear of France. England foresaw with terror the opening of another era of Napoleonic conquest, and it was with divided sympathies that she watched the Lombard campaign of 1859. The battles of Magenta and Solferino liberated Lombardy from Austria, and rendered the liberation of the rest of Italy possible in the near future.

The confusion of the English mind on the subject

of the war of 1859 has been satirised by Matthew
Arnold in *Friendship's Garland,* and by Ruskin in
Arrows of the Chase. It would not be untrue to say
that Englishmen hoped the Austrians would beat the
French, and that the Piedmontese would beat the
Austrians. What net result they wished to come out
of the war they would scarcely have been able to
explain ; but the result that actually emerged was
admirably suited to fulfil English wishes and to pro-
mote English policy.

One British citizen, a poetess living in Florence,
regarded her countrymen unequivocally as Pharisees,
because they would rather see Italy rest enslaved than
freed by the man whom they regarded as their enemy ;
and risking her great popularity, Mrs. Browning told
them so to their face. ' If patriotism,' she wrote in
the Preface to her *Poems before Congress,* ' means the
flattery of one's nation in every case, then the patriot,
take it as you please, is merely the courtier ; which I
am not, though I have written *Napoleon III. in Italy.*'
In that poem she praised and thanked the French
emperor as the liberator of Italy, ascribed to him
purely generous motives, and hailed him as ' Emperor
evermore,' in spite of the crime of the *coup d'état*
which had won him his throne, and in spite of the
opposition of the French and European Liberals with
whom she was otherwise in general sympathy. This
highly controversial poem, which does credit to her
courage and sincerity, because it was published in
defiance of all the good and bad prejudices of her
countrymen, is perhaps about as far removed from the

truth as is the completely hostile view of Napoleon that satisfied Mazzini and the English. Both his character and his policy were more composite of good and evil than either Mrs. Browning, on the one hand, or her countrymen on the other, were at all aware. There was only one man in Europe who thoroughly understood Napoleon and his position. That man was not himself but Cavour, whose grand task during the last three years of his life was the exploitation of the French emperor.

The sudden termination of the Lombard campaign of 1859, by the useful but disappointing Treaty of Villafranca, ended the honeymoon of France and Italy which Mrs. Browning had blessed, and threw Italy into the arms of England. The new Liberal Government, with Lord John Russell as Foreign Minister, was not slow to seize the opportunity. English interests were served by the disinterested feeling for the Italian cause prevailing over here, to which there was very little corresponding in French public opinion except in one corner of Napoleon's own heart. The English Press took up the cause of United Italy, pointed out to the Italians that Napoleon was but a half-hearted friend, and began to idolise Garibaldi as the enemy of Napoleon and of Austria alike. Cavour let England and France bid against each other for Italy's favour, and seized the opportunity, with Garibaldi's help, to make the Italian kingdom.

The year 1860, celebrated in Swinburne's poem *In Time of Revolution*, saw the liberation of Sicily and Naples by the great adventure of Garibaldi, and the consequent liberation of Papal Umbria and the Marches by the regular army of Victor Emmanuel. The immediate outcome was the United Kingdom of Italy, formed against the wishes of all the great European powers except England, who was the first to recognise the new State in the spring of 1861.

Mrs. Browning died at Florence in the following summer, having seen her dream realised for all Italy except Rome and Venice. At the time of her death the English poet whose name will live longest in connection with the theme of Italian liberty was only beginning to express in verse the enthusiasm for that cause which was to inspire half his finest work. Swinburne's devotion to Italy was not, like that of Byron or the Brownings, the result of knowledge of the Italians and understanding of their problems. It was inspired by Mazzini's cast-iron Republican theories, already dead as a practical influence on the world of Italian politics, but resuscitated into immortal life by their adaptation to the art and temperament of his singular disciple. It may be doubted whether the poet of such a headlong river of song, fresh and glorious as Arethusa springing from her couch of snows, could have halted to think, without losing more in volume and simplicity than could have been replaced by greater penetration or breadth of outlook. In the Muses' house are many mansions. When a great poet thinks deeply on historical and political subjects, like Meredith in his *Odes on French History*, he may achieve something unique, but he is not likely to attain to the lyrical splendour of Swinburne's *Songs before Sunrise*.

The *Monotones* of Mazzini's unbending faith were admirably suited to produce the full genius of Swinburne.

> 'Because there is but one truth;
> Because there is but one banner;
> Because there is but one light;
> Because we have with us our youth
> Once, and one chance and one manner
> Of service, and then the night.' *

To this later period of the *Risorgimento* belongs the poetic genius of Carducci, who represents to his countrymen the finest spirit of their nation. Meredith may well have been thinking of Carducci's popularity with his own people when he said, on Swinburne's death, that if Swinburne had been an Italian he would have been hailed as the National Poet.

In 1866 Italy acquired Venice, and in 1870 Rome. The dream for which Shelley had scarcely dared to hope in his vision on the Euganean Hills, the 'free Italy' for which Byron had been so willing to sacrifice himself, became an accomplished and thereupon a most prosaic fact. Even while I write these words the prospect is arising that Italy will of her own accord throw away the one inestimable advantage that she has hitherto had over the other Great Powers, of being the conqueror of no other race, and mistress only in her own house. The warship *Garibaldi*,

---

* This volume would not be worth publishing but for the generosity of Mr. Watts Dunton in allowing me to make such free use of his copyrights.

one reads, is bombarding Tripoli. It is not hard to guess what the namesake of that ship would have thought of this attack upon the liberty of others.

The ' red, white, and green ' has become one of the least honourable of the ' commercial assets ' waving over a militarist and financial Europe. Yet sometimes, somewhere, for a little, ideals stir the masses of men, and at all times the tourist in Italy will do well to remember that but sixty years ago it was death to show those three colours, that the thought of the hidden flag was the sacrament of a great faith and of a pure and mighty brotherhood, and that English poets, the like of whom are no longer found in the world, felt their hearts throb at the sight of that foreign flag, and hailed it as

> ' a beacon beneath to the beacon above,
> Green as our hope in it, white as our faith in it, red as
> our love.'

CONTENTS

ENGLISH SONGS OF ITALIAN FREEDOM

CONTENTS

ENGLISH SONGS
OF ITALIAN FREEDOM

Shelley

LINES WRITTEN AMONG THE
EUGANEAN HILLS

OCTOBER 1818

[An isolated group of hills, the Euganean, the shape of which is familiar to every one who has traversed the Venetian lagoons, rises out of the flat level of the Lombard plain about thirty miles west of Venice. Their rounded summits command the finest of all views of the plain of Lombardy, in which they form, as it were, islands, midway between the enclosing shores of Alps to north and Apennines to south. A near prospect of the city of Padua, and a more distant and romantic vision of the campaniles of sea-girt Venice standing out against the sunrise and the line of the Adriatic, complete the view from the Euganean hills which inspired Shelley to write this poem. At that time, three years after Waterloo, the ancient republic of Venice and the whole Lombard plain between Adriatic and Milan were held in subjection 'under the mighty Austrian' whose Teutonic and Magyar hordes are more than once spoken of in this poem as 'Celts,' through what ethnological error of fancy on Shelley's part I cannot conceive. His companion Byron preferred to speak of the transalpine tyrants of Italy as 'the Barbarians.' For remarks on Byron and Shelley in Italy see p. xvi above, in the Introduction.]

MANY a green isle needs must be
    In the deep wide sea of Misery ;
Or the mariner, worn and wan,
Never thus could voyage on—

Day and night, and night and day,
Drifting on his dreary way,
With the solid darkness black
Closing round his vessel's track ;
Whilst, above, the sunless sky,
Big with clouds, hangs heavily—
And, behind, the tempest fleet
Hurries on with lightning feet,
Riving sail and cord and plank,
Till the ship has almost drank
Death from the o'er-brimming deep,
And sinks down, down, like that sleep
When the dreamer seems to be
Weltering through eternity,
And the dim low line before
Of a dark and distant shore
Still recedes, as—ever still
Longing with divided will,
But no power to seek or shun—
He is ever drifted on
O'er the unreposing wave
To the haven of the grave.
What if there no friends will greet !
What if there no heart will meet
His with love's impatient beat ?
Wander wheresoe'er he may,
Can he dream before that day
To find refuge from distress
In friendship's smile, in love's caress ?
Then 'twill wreak him little woe
Whether such there be or no.
Senseless is the breast, and cold,

Which relenting love would fold ;
Bloodless are the veins, and chill,
Which the pulse of pain did fill ;
Every little living nerve
That from bitter words did swerve
Round the tortured lips and brow
Are like sapless leaflets now
Frozen upon December's bough.

On the beach of a northern sea
Which tempests shake eternally
As once the wretch there lay to sleep,
Lies a solitary heap,
One white skull and seven dry bones,
On the margin of the stones,
Where a few grey rushes stand,
Boundaries of the sea and land.
Nor is heard one voice of wail
But the sea-mews' as they sail
O'er the billows of the gale,
Or the whirlwind up and down
Howling—like a slaughtered town,
Where a king in glory rides
Through the pomp of fratricides.
Those unburied bones around
There is many a mournful sound ;
There is no lament for him,
Like a sunless vapour, dim,
Who once clothed with life and thought
What now moves nor murmurs not.

Ay, many flowering islands lie
In the waters of wide Agony :

3

To such a one this morn was led
My bark, by soft winds piloted.
'Mid the mountains Euganean,
I stood listening to the pæan
With which the legioned rooks did hail
The sun's uprise majestical.
Gathering round with wings all hoar,
Through the dewy mist they soar
Like grey shades, till the eastern heaven
Bursts ; and then, as clouds of even
Flecked with fire and azure lie
In the unfathomable sky,
So their plumes of purple grain,
Starred with drops of golden rain,
Gleam above the sunlight woods,
As in silent multitudes
On the morning's fitful gale
Through the broken mist they sail,
And the vapours cloven and gleaming
Follow, down the dark steep streaming—
Till all is bright, and clear, and still
Round the solitary hill.

Beneath is spread like a green sea
The waveless plain of Lombardy,
Bounded by the vaporous air,
Islanded by cities fair.
Underneath Day's azure eyes,
Ocean's nursling, Venice lies—
A peopled labyrinth of walls,
Amphitrite's destined halls,

Which her hoary sire now paves
With his blue and beaming waves.
Lo ! the sun upsprings behind,
Broad, red, radiant, half-reclined
On the level quivering line
Of the waters crystalline ;
And before that chasm of light,
As within a furnace bright,
Column, tower, and dome, and spire,
Shine like obelisks of fire,
Pointing with inconstant motion
From the altar of dark ocean
To the sapphire-tinted skies ;
As the flames of sacrifice
From the marble shrines did rise,
As to pierce the dome of gold
Where Apollo spoke of old.

Sun-girt City ! thou hast been
Ocean's child, and then his queen.
Now is come a darker day,
And thou soon must be his prey,
If the power that raised thee here
Hallow so thy watery bier.[1]
A less drear ruin then than now,
With thy conquest-branded brow
Stooping to the slave of slaves
From thy throne, among the waves
Wilt thou be when the sea-mew
Flies, as once before it flew,
O'er thine isles depopulate,
And all is in its ancient state ;

Save where many a palace gate
With green sea-flowers overgrown
Like a rock of ocean's own,
Topples o'er the abandoned sea
As the tides change sullenly.
The fisher on his watery way
Wandering at the close of day
Will spread his sail and seize his oar
Till he pass the gloomy shore,
Lest thy dead should, from their sleep
Bursting o'er the starlight deep,
Lead a rapid masque of death
O'er the waters of his path.

Those who alone thy towers behold
Quivering through aërial gold,
As I now behold them here,
Would imagine not they were
Sepulchres where human forms,
Like pollution-nourished worms,
To the corpse of greatness cling,
Murdered and now mouldering.
But, if Freedom should awake
In her omnipotence, and shake
From the Celtic Anarch's hold
All the keys of dungeons cold
Where a hundred cities lie
Chained like thee ingloriously,
Thou and all thy sister band
Might adorn this sunny land,
Twining memories of old time
With new virtues more sublime.

If not, perish thou and they—
Clouds which stain truth's rising day,
By her sun consumed away!
Earth can spare ye; while like flowers,
In the waste of years and hours,
From your dust new nations spring
With more kindly blossoming.

Perish! Let there only be,
Floating o'er thy heartless sea
As the garment of thy sky
Clothes the world immortally,
One remembrance, more sublime
Than the tattered pall of time
Which scarce hides thy visage wan :
That a tempest-cleaving swan
Of the songs of Albion,
Driven from his ancestral streams
By the might of evil dreams,
Found a nest in thee ; [2] and ocean
Welcomed him with such emotion
That its joy grew his, and sprung
From his lips like music flung
O'er a mighty thunder-fit,
Chastening terror. What though yet
Poesy's unfailing river,
Which through Albion winds for ever,
Lashing with melodious wave
Many a sacred poet's grave,
Mourn its latest nursling fled ?
What though thou with all thy dead

Scarce canst for this fame repay
Aught thine own—oh! rather say,
Though thy sins and slaveries foul
Overcloud a sunlike soul? [3]
As the ghost of Homer clings
Round Scamander's wasting springs;
As divinest Shakespeare's might
Fills Avon and the world with light,
Like Omniscient Power, which he
Imaged 'mid mortality;
As the love from Petrarch's urn
Yet amid yon hills doth burn,
A quenchless lamp by which the heart
Sees things unearthly; so thou art,
Mighty spirit! so shall be
The city that did refuge thee! [4]

Lo, the sun floats up the sky,
Like thought-wingèd Liberty,
Till the universal light
Seems to level plain and height.
From the sea a mist has spread,
And the beams of morn lie dead
On the towers of Venice now,
Like its glory long ago.
By the skirts of that grey cloud
Many-domèd Padua proud
Stands, a peopled solitude
'Mid the harvest-shining plain;
Where the peasant heaps his grain
In the garner of his foe,[5]
And the milk-white oxen slow

With the purple vintage strain
Heaped upon the creaking wain,
That the brutal Celt may swill
Drunken sleep with savage will.
And the sickle to the sword
Lies unchanged, though many a lord,
Like a weed whose shade is poison,
Overgrows this region's foison,
Sheaves of whom are ripe to come
To destruction's harvest-home.
Men must reap the things they sow ;
Force from force must ever flow,
Or worse : but 'tis a bitter woe
That love or reason cannot change
The despot's rage, the slave's revenge.

Padua, thou within whose walls
Those mute guests at festivals,
Son and Mother, Death and Sin,
Played at dice for Ezzelin,⁶
Till Death cried, ' I win, I win ! '
And Sin cursed to lose the wager ;
But Death promised, to assuage her,
That he would petition for
Her to be made Vice-Emperor,
When the destined years were o'er,
Over all between the Po
And the eastern Alpine snow,
Under the mighty Austrian :
Sin smiled so as Sin only can ;
And, since that time, ay long before
Both have ruled from shore to shore,

9

That incestuous pair who follow
Tyrants as the sun the swallow,
As repentance follows crime,
And as changes follow time.

In thine halls the lamp of learning,
Padua, now no more is burning.[7]
Like a meteor whose wild way
Is lost over the grave of day,
It gleams betrayed and to betray.
Once remotest nations came
To adore that sacred flame,
When it lit not many a hearth
On this cold and gloomy earth ;
Now new fires from antique light
Spring beneath the wide world's might—
But their spark lies dead in thee,
Trampled out by Tyranny.
As the Norway woodman quells,
In the depth of piny dells,
One light flame among the brakes,
While the boundless forest shakes,
And its mighty trunks are torn
By the fire thus lowly born—
The spark beneath his feet is dead ;
He starts to see the flames it fed
Howling through the darkened sky
With myriad tongues victoriously,
And sinks down in fear—so thou,
O Tyranny ! beholdest now
Light around thee, and thou hearest
The loud flames ascend, and fearest.

SHELLEY

Grovel on the earth ! ay, hide
In the dust thy purple pride !

Noon descends around me now,
'Tis the noon of autumn's glow ;
When a soft and purple mist,
Like a vaporous amethyst,
Or an air-dissolvèd star
Mingling light and fragrance, far
From the curved horizon's bound
To the point of heaven's profound
Fills the overflowing sky.
And the plains that silent lie
Underneath ; the leaves unsodden
Where the infant Frost has trodden
With his morning-wingèd feet
Whose bright print is gleaming yet ;
And the red and golden vines,
Piercing with their trellised lines
The rough dark-skirted wilderness ;
The dun and bladed grass no less,
Pointing from this hoary tower
In the windless air ; the flower
Glimmering at my feet ; the line
Of the olive-sandalled Apennine
In the south dimly islanded ;
And the Alps, whose snows are spread
High between the clouds and sun ;
And of living things each one ;
And my spirit, which so long
Darkened this swift stream of song—

Interpenetrated lie
By the glory of the sky :
Be it love, light, harmony,
Odour, or the soul of all
Which from heaven like dew doth fall,
Or the mind which feeds this verse
Peopling the lone universe.

Noon descends ; and after noon
Autumn's evening meets me soon,
Leading the infantine moon,
And that one star which to her
Almost seems to minister
Half the crimson light she brings
From the sunset's radiant springs.
And the soft dreams of the morn
(Which like winged winds had borne
To that silent isle which lies
'Mid remembered agonies,
The frail bark of this lone being)
Pass, to other sufferers fleeing ;
And its ancient pilot, Pain,
Sits beside the helm again.
Other flowering isles must be
In the sea of Life and Agony :
Other spirits float and flee
O'er that gulf.   Even now perhaps
On some rock the wild wave wraps,
With folded wings, they waiting sit
For my bark, to pilot it
To some calm and blooming cove ;
Where for me and those I love

SHELLEY

May a windless bower be built,
Far from passion, pain, and guilt,
In a dell 'mid lawny hills
Which the wild sea-murmur fills,
And soft sunshine, and the sound
Of old forests echoing round,
And the light and smell divine
Of all flowers that breathe and shine.
We may live so happy there
That the Spirits of the Air,
Envying us, may even entice
To our healing paradise
The polluting multitude.
But their rage would be subdued
By that clime divine and calm,
And the winds whose wings rain balm
On the uplifted soul, and leaves
Under which the bright sea heaves ;
While each breathless interval
In their whisperings musical
The inspirèd soul supplies
With its own deep melodies,
And the love which heals all strife,
Circling, like the breath of life,
All things in that sweet abode
With its own mild brotherhood.
They, not it, would change ; and soon
Every sprite beneath the moon
Would repent its envy vain,
And the earth grow young again.

Byron

CHILDE HAROLD'S PILGRIMAGE. CANTO IV.

[In the same year, 1818, while Shelley mourned over the slavery
of Venice in the 'Lines written among the Euganean Hills,' Byron
expressed similar sentiments to a larger English and European
public in his famous 'Fourth Canto of Childe Harold,' of which
the following stanzas are germane to the subject of this volume.]

I STOOD in Venice, on the Bridge of Sighs ;
   A palace and a prison on each hand :
I saw from out the wave her structures rise
As from the stroke of the enchanter's wand :
A thousand years their cloudy wings expand
Around me, and a dying Glory smiles
O'er the far times, when many a subject land
Look'd to the winged Lion's marble piles,
Where Venice sate in state, throned on her hundred isles !

She looks a sea Cybele, fresh from ocean,
Rising with her tiara of proud towers
At airy distance, with majestic motion,
A ruler of the waters and their powers :
And such she was ;—her daughters had their dowers
From spoils of nations, and the exhaustless East
Pour'd in her lap all gems in sparkling showers.
In purple was she robed, and of her feast
Monarchs partook, and deem'd their dignity increased.

14

BYRON

In Venice Tasso's echoes are no more,
And silent rows the songless gondolier;
Her palaces are crumbling to the shore,
And music meets not always now the ear:
Those days are gone—but Beauty still is here.
States fall, arts fade—but Nature doth not die,
Nor yet forget how Venice once was dear,
The pleasant place of all festivity,
The revel of the earth, the masque of Italy!
 *   *   *   *   *   *   *

The spouseless Adriatic mourns her lord;
And, annual marriage now no more renew'd,
The Bucentaur lies rotting unrestored,
Neglected garment of her widowhood!
St. Mark yet sees his lion where he stood
Stand, but in mockery of his wither'd power,
Over the proud Place where an Emperor sued,
And monarchs gazed and envied in the hour
When Venice was a queen with an unequall'd dower.

The Suabian sued, and now the Austrian reigns—
An Emperor tramples where an Emperor knelt;
Kingdoms are shrunk to provinces, and chains
Clank over sceptred cities; nations melt
From power's high pinnacle, when they have felt
The sunshine for a while, and downward go
Like lauwine loosen'd from the mountain's belt;
Oh for one hour of blind old Dandolo!
Th' octogenarian chief, Byzantium's conquering foe.

Before St. Mark still glow his steeds of brass,
Their gilded collars glittering in the sun; [1]
But is not Doria's menace come to pass?

Are they not *bridled* ?—Venice, lost and won,
Her thirteen hundred years of freedom done,
Sinks, like a seaweed, into whence she rose !
Better be whelm'd beneath the waves, and shun,
Even in destruction's depth, her foreign foes,
From whom submission wrings an infamous repose.

  * * * * * * *

Italia ! oh Italia ! thou who hast
The fatal gift of beauty, which became
A funeral dower of present woes and past,
On thy sweet brow is sorrow plough'd by shame,
And annals graved in characters of flame.
Oh, God ! that thou wert in thy nakedness
Less lovely or more powerful, and couldst claim
Thy right, and awe the robbers back, who press
To shed thy blood, and drink the tears of thy distress ;

Then might'st thou more appal ; or, less desired,
Be homely and be peaceful, undeplored
For thy destructive charms ; then, still untired,
Would not be seen the armed torrents pour'd
Down the deep Alps ; nor would the hostile horde
Of many-nation'd spoilers from the Po
Quaff blood and water ; nor the stranger's sword
Be thy sad weapon of defence, and so,
Victor or vanquish'd, thou the slave of friend or foe.[2]

  * * * * * * *

Yet, Italy ! through every other land
Thy wrongs should ring, and shall, from side to side ;
Mother of Arts ! as once of arms ; thy hand
Was then our guardian, and is still our guide ;
Parent of our religion ! whom the wide

Nations have knelt to for the keys of heaven !
Europe, repentant of her parricide,
Shall yet redeem thee, and, all backward driven,
Roll the barbarian tide, and sue to be forgiven.

 *   *   *   *   *   *   *

O Rome ! my country ! city of the soul !
The orphans of the heart must turn to thee,
Lone mother of dead empires ! and control
In their shut breasts their petty misery.
What are our woes and sufferance ? Come and see
The cypress, hear the owl, and plod your way
O'er steps of broken thrones and temples, Ye !
Whose agonies are evils of a day—
A world is at our feet as fragile as our clay.

The Niobe of nations ! there she stands,
Childless and crownless, in her voiceless woe ;
An empty urn within her wither'd hands,
Whose holy dust was scatter'd long ago ;
The Scipios' tomb contains no ashes now ;
The very sepulchres lie tenantless
Of their heroic dwellers : dost thou flow,
Old Tiber ! through a marble wilderness ?
Rise, with thy yellow waves, and mantle her distress.

The Goths, the Christian, Time, War, Flood, and
  Fire,
Have dealt upon the seven-hill'd city's pride ;
She saw her glories star by star expire,
And up the steep barbarian monarchs ride,
Where the car climb'd the Capitol ; far and wide
Temple and tower went down, nor left a site :

Chaos of ruins ! who shall trace the void,
O'er the dim fragments cast a lunar light,
And say, ' Here was, or is,' where all is doubly night ?

The double night of ages, and of her,
Night's daughter, Ignorance, hath wrapt and wrap
All round us ; we but feel our way to err :
The ocean hath its chart, the stars their map,
And Knowledge spreads them on her ample lap ;
But Rome is as the desert, where we steer
Stumbling o'er recollections ; now we clap
Our hands, and cry ' Eureka ! ' it is clear—
When but some false mirage of ruin rises near.

Alas ! the lofty city ! and alas !
The trebly hundred triumphs ! and the day
When Brutus made the dagger's edge surpass
The conqueror's sword in bearing fame away !
Alas, for Tully's voice, and Virgil's lay,
And Livy's pictured page !—but these shall be
Her resurrection ; all beside—decay.
Alas, for Earth, for never shall we see
That brightness in her eye she bore when Rome was free !

Oh thou, whose chariot roll'd on Fortune's wheel,
Triumphant Sylla ! Thou, who didst subdue
Thy country's foes ere thou wouldst pause to feel
The wrath of thy own wrongs, or reap the due
Of hoarded vengeance till thine eagles flew
O'er prostrate Asia ;—thou, who with thy frown
Annihilated senates—Roman, too,
With all thy vices, for thou didst lay down
With an atoning smile a more than earthly crown—

BYRON

The dictatorial wreath—couldst thou divine
To what would one day dwindle that which made
Thee more than mortal ? and that so supine
By aught than Romans Rome should thus be laid ?
She who was named Eternal, and array'd
Her warriors but to conquer—she who veil'd
Earth with her haughty shadow, and display'd,
Until the o'er-canopied horizon fail'd,
Her rushing wings—Oh! she who was Almighty
    hail'd !

   *   *   *   *   *   *   *

What from this barren being do we reap ?
Our senses narrow, and our reason frail,
Life short, and truth a gem which loves the deep.
And all things weigh'd in custom's falsest scale ;
Opinion an omnipotence,—whose veil
Mantles the earth with darkness, until right
And wrong are accidents, and men grow pale
Lest their own judgments should become too bright,
And their free thoughts be crimes, and earth have too
    much light.

And thus they plod in sluggish misery,
Rotting from sire to son, and age to age,
Proud of their trampled nature, and so die,
Bequeathing their hereditary rage
To the new race of inborn slaves, who wage
War for their chains, and rather than be free,
Bleed gladiator-like, and still engage
Within the same arena where they see
Their fellows fall before, like leaves of the same tree.

I speak not of men's creeds—they rest between
Man and his Maker—but of things allow'd,
Averr'd, and known, and daily, hourly seen—
The yoke that is upon us doubly bow'd,
And the intent of tyranny avow'd,
The edict of Earth's rulers, who are grown
The apes of him who humbled once the proud,
And shook them from their slumbers on the throne :
Too glorious, were this all his mighty arm had done.[3]

Can tyrants but by tyrants conquer'd be,
And freedom find no champion and no child
Such as Columbia saw arise when she
Sprung forth a Pallas, arm'd and undefiled ?
Or must such minds be nourish'd in the wild,
Deep in the unpruned forest, 'midst the roar
Of cataracts, where nursing Nature smiled
On infant Washington ?   Has Earth no more
Such seeds within her breast, or Europe no such shore ?

But France got drunk with blood to vomit crime,
And fatal have her Saturnalia been
To Freedom's cause, in every age and clime ;
Because the deadly days which we have seen,
And vile Ambition, that built up between
Man and his hopes an adamantine wall,
And the base pageant last upon the scene,
Are grown the pretext for the eternal thrall
Which nips life's tree, and dooms man's worst—his second
        fall.

BYRON

Yet, Freedom ! yet thy banner, torn, but flying,
Streams like the thunder-storm *against* the wind ;
Thy trumpet voice, though broken now and dying,
The loudest still the tempest leaves behind ;
Thy tree hath lost its blossoms, and the rind,
Chopp'd by the axe, looks rough and little worth,
But the sap lasts,—and still the seed we find
Sown deep, even in the bosom of the North ;
So shall a better spring less bitter fruit bring forth.
*   *   *   *   *   *   *

Byron

ODE ON VENICE

[In the same year (1818) Byron wrote the following *Ode on Venice*. The year 1818 was perhaps the year of the most hopeless servitude of Europe to the principles of the Holy Alliance and to Metternich's conception of 'order,' and in this poem Byron's despair of liberty in Europe seems almost unrelieved by the hopes that called him to action a few years later.]

I

OH Venice ! Venice ! when thy marble walls
    Are level with the waters, there shall be
A cry of nations o'er thy sunken halls,
    A loud lament along the sweeping sea !
If I, a northern wanderer, weep for thee,
What should thy sons do ?—anything but weep :
And yet they only murmur in their sleep.
In contrast with their fathers—as the slime,
The dull green ooze of the receding deep,
Is with the dashing of the spring-tide foam
That drives the sailor shipless to his home,
Are they to those that were ; and thus they creep,
Crouching and crab-like, through their sapping streets.
Oh ! agony—that centuries should reap
No mellower harvest ! Thirteen hundred years
Of wealth and glory turn'd to dust and tears,
And every monument the stranger meets,
Church, palace, pillar, as a mourner greets ;
And even the Lion all subdued appears,

22

And the harsh sound of the barbarian drum,[1]
With dull and daily dissonance, repeats
The echo of thy tyrant's voice along
The soft waves, once all musical to song,
That heaved beneath the moonlight with the throng
Of gondolas—and to the busy hum
Of cheerful creatures, whose most sinful deeds
Were but the overbeating of the heart,
And flow of too much happiness, which needs
The aid of age to turn its course apart
From the luxuriant and voluptuous flood
Of sweet sensations, battling with the blood.
But these are better than the gloomy errors,
The weeds of nations in their last decay,
When Vice walks forth with her unsoften'd terrors,
And Mirth is madness, and but smiles to slay ;
And Hope is nothing but a false delay,
The sick man's lightning half an hour ere death,
When Faintness, the last mortal birth of Pain,
And apathy of limb, the dull beginning
Of the cold staggering race which Death is winning,
Steals vein by vein and pulse by pulse away ;
Yet so relieving the o'er-tortured clay,
To him appears renewal of his breath,
And freedom the mere numbness of his chain ;
And then he talks of life, and how again
He feels his spirits soaring—albeit weak,
And of the fresher air, which he would seek :
And as he whispers knows not that he gasps,
That his thin finger feels not what it clasps,
And so the film comes o'er him, and the dizzy
Chamber swims round and round, and shadows busy,

At which he vainly catches, flit and gleam,
Till the last rattle chokes the strangled scream,
And all is ice and blackness,—and the earth
That which it was the moment ere our birth.

II

There is no hope for nations !—Search the page
  Of many thousand years—the daily scene,
The flow and ebb of each recurring age,
  The everlasting *to be* which *hath been*,
  Hath taught us nought, or little : still we lean
On things that rot beneath our weight, and wear
Our strength away in wrestling with the air :
For 'tis our nature strikes us down : the beasts
Slaughter'd in hourly hecatombs for feasts
Are of as high an order—they must go
Even where their driver goads them, though to
  slaughter.
Ye men, who pour your blood for kings as water,
What have they given your children in return ? [2]
A heritage of servitude and woes,
A blindfold bondage, where your hire is blows.
What ! do not yet the red-hot ploughshares burn,
O'er which you stumble in a false ordeal,
And deem this proof of loyalty the *real* ;
Kissing the hand that guides you to your scars,
And glorying as you tread the glowing bars ?
All that your sires have left you, all that Time
Bequeaths of free, and History of sublime,
Spring from a different theme ! Ye see and read,
Admire and sigh, and then succumb and bleed !

BYRON

Save the few spirits who, despite of all,
And worse than all, the sudden crimes engender'd
By the down-thundering of the prison-wall,
And thirst to swallow the sweet waters tender'd,
Gushing from Freedom's fountains, when the crowd,
Madden'd with centuries of drought, are loud,
And trample on each other to obtain
The cup which brings oblivion of a chain
Heavy and sore, in which long yoked they plough'd
The sand,—or if there sprung the yellow grain,
'Twas not for them, their necks were too much bow'd,
And their dead palates chew'd the cud of pain :
Yes ! the few spirits, who, despite of deeds
Which they abhor, confound not with the cause
Those momentary starts from Nature's laws,
Which, like the pestilence and earthquake, smite
But for a term, then pass, and leave the earth
With all her seasons to repair the blight
With a few summers, and again put forth
Cities and generations—fair, when free—
For, Tyranny, there blooms no bud for thee !

III

Glory and Empire ! once upon these towers
  With Freedom—godlike Triad ! how ye sate !
The league of mightiest nations, in those hours
  When Venice was an envy, might abate,
  But did not quench her spirit,[3] in her fate
All were enwrapp'd : the feasted monarchs knew
  And loved their hostess, nor could learn to hate,
Although they humbled—with the kingly few

The many felt, for from all days and climes
She was the voyager's worship ; even her crimes
Were of the softer order—born of love,
She drank no blood, nor fatten'd on the dead,
But gladden'd where her harmless conquests spread ;
For these restored the Cross, that from above
Hallow'd her sheltering banners, which incessant
Flew between earth and the unholy Crescent,
Which, if it waned and dwindled, Earth may thank
The city it has clothed in chains, which clank
Now, creaking in the ears of those who owe
The name of Freedom to her glorious struggles ;
Yet she but shares with them a common woe,
And call'd the ' kingdom ' of a conquering foe,
But knows what all—and, most of all, *we* know—
With what set gilded terms a tyrant juggles !
The name of Commonwealth is past and gone
   O'er the three fractions of the groaning globe ;
Venice is crush'd, and Holland deigns to own
   A sceptre, and endures the purple robe ;
If the free Switzer yet bestrides alone
His chainless mountains, 'tis but for a time,
For tyranny of late is cunning grown,
And in its own good season tramples down
The sparkles of our ashes.   One great clime,
Whose vigorous offspring by dividing ocean
Are kept apart and nursed in the devotion
Of Freedom, which their fathers fought for, and
Bequeath'd—a heritage of heart and hand,
And proud distinction from each other land,
Whose sons must bow them at a monarch's motion
As if his senseless sceptre were a wand

BYRON

Full of the magic of exploded science—
Still one great clime, in full and free defiance,
Yet rears her crest, unconquer'd and sublime,
Above the far Atlantic !—She has taught
Her Esau-brethren that the haughty flag,
The floating fence of Albion's feebler crag,
May strike to those whose red right hands have bought
Rights cheaply earn'd with blood.   Still, still, for ever,
Better, though each man's life-blood were a river,
That it should flow, and overflow, than creep
Through thousand lazy channels in our veins,
Damm'd like the dull canal with locks and chains,
And moving, as a sick man in his sleep,
Three paces, and then faltering : better be
Where the extinguish'd Spartans still are free,
In their proud charnel of Thermopylæ,
Than stagnate in our marsh,—or o'er the deep
Fly, and one current to the ocean add,
One spirit to the souls our fathers had,
One freeman more, America, to thee !

Shelley

ODE TO NAPLES

1820

[The revolution of July 1820, whereby the *carbonari* and the army of the Neapolitan Kingdom extorted a constitution from their Bourbon monarch, was the first movement of the Italian *risorgimento* after the fall of Napoleon. For its effect upon the rest of Italy and on Byron and Shelley see Introduction, p. xvii above. It inspired this poem, written by Shelley near Pisa in Tuscan territory, while a constitutional government actually existed at Naples and while the rest of Italy was seething with agitation and hope, as described in Antistrophe *a c.*

In Epode I. *a* and II. *a* the poet recalls his recent visit to the Bay of Naples, now become the scene of events that so deeply stir him ; the 'city disinterred' of the first line is of course Pompeii. The 'bloodless sacrifice' which he praises in Strophe *a* I is the recent Neapolitan revolution which had indeed been singularly innocent and bloodless. In this, as in much else, it resembled the liberal revolution recently effected by the army in Spain—an event which had been the example inspiring the Neapolitan liberal leaders, and which is referred to in the first line of Antistrophe *a c.*

In Epode I. *b* Shelley describes the Austrian army coming over the Alpine passes and marching down the length of Italy to suppress the Neapolitan constitution at the orders of the Holy Alliance.

In Epode II. *b* he hopes that the Italians, 'the Ausonian shepherds,' will chase the Austrians, 'the Celtic wolves.' Unfortunately the wolves speedily chased the shepherds.]

EPODE I. *a*

I STOOD within the city disinterred ;
    And heard the autumnal leaves like light footfalls
Of spirits passing through the streets ; and heard
    The Mountain's slumberous voice at intervals
        Thrill through those roofless halls.

The oracular thunder penetrating shook
  The listening soul in my suspended blood ;
  I felt that Earth out of her deep heart spoke—
  I felt, but heard not.   Through white columns glowed
    The isle-sustaining ocean-flood,
A plane of light between two heavens of azure.
  Around me gleamed many a bright sepulchre,
Of whose pure beauty Time, as if his pleasure
Were to spare Death, had never made erasure ;
  But every living lineament was clear
      As in the sculptor's thought, and there
The wreaths of stony myrtle, ivy, and pine,
      Like winter leaves o'ergrown by moulded snow,
      Seemed only not to move and grow
Because the crystal silence of the air
Weighed on their life, even as the Power divine
Which then lulled all things brooded upon mine.

EPODE II. a

      Then gentle winds arose,
      With many a mingled close
Of wild Æolian sound and mountain odour keen.
      And where the Baian ocean
      Welters, with air-like motion,
Within, above, around its bowers of starry green,
    Moving the sea-flowers in those purple caves,
      Even as the ever stormless atmosphere
      Floats o'er the elysian realm,
    It bore me like an angel, o'er the waves
    Of sunlight, whose swift pinnace of dewy air
      No storm can overwhelm.
      I sailed where ever flows

Under the calm serene
A spirit of deep emotion
From the unknown graves
Of the dead kings of melody.
Shadowy Aornos darkened o'er the helm
The horizontal ether ; heaven stripped bare
Its depths over Elysium, where the prow
Made the invisible water white as snow ;
From that Typhæan mount, Inarime,
There streamed a sunlit vapour, like the standard
Of some ethereal host ;
Whilst from all the coast,
Louder and louder, gathering round, there wandered
Over the oracular woods and divine sea
Prophesyings which grew articulate—
They seize me—I must speak them—be they fate !

STROPHE *a* I

Naples ! thou heart of men which ever pantest
Naked beneath the lidless eye of heaven !
Elsyian City, which to calm enchantest
The mutinous air and sea—they round thee, even
As Sleep round Love, are driven !
Metropolis of a ruined paradise
Long lost, late won, and yet but half regained !
Bright altar of the bloodless sacrifice
Which armèd Victory offers up unstained
To Love the flower-enchained !
Thou which wert once, and then didst cease to be,
Now art, and henceforth ever shalt be, free,
If Hope, and Truth, and Justice can avail—
Hail, hail, all hail !

SHELLEY

Thou youngest giant birth
Which from the groaning earth
Leap'st, clothed in armour of impenetrable scale !
Last of the intercessors
Who 'gainst the crowned transgressors
Pleadest before God's love ! arrayed in wisdom's mail,
Wave thy lightning lance in mirth ;
Nor let thy high heart fail,
Though from their hundred gates the leagued
oppressors
With hurried legions move ! Hail, hail, all hail !

ANTISTROPHE *a*

What though Cimmerian Anarchs dare blaspheme
Freedom and thee ? Thy shield is as a mirror
To make their blind slaves see, and with fierce gleam
To turn his hungry sword upon the wearer ;
A new Actæon's error
Shall theirs have been—devoured by their own hounds!
Be thou like the imperial basilisk,
Killing thy foe with unapparent wounds !
Gaze on Oppression, till, at that dread risk
Aghast, she pass from the earth's disk ;
Fear not, but gaze—for freemen mightier grow,
And slaves more feeble, gazing on their foe.
If Hope, and Truth, and Justice may avail,
Thou shalt be great.—All hail !

ANTISTROPHE *b* 2

From Freedom's form divine,
From Nature's inmost shrine,

Strip every impious gawd, rend error veil by veil :
    O'er Ruin desolate,
    O'er Falsehood's fallen state,
Sit thou sublime, unawed ; be the Destroyer pale !
    And equal laws be thine,
    And wingèd words let sail,
Freighted with truth even from the throne of God !
That wealth, surviving fate, be thine.—All hail !

ANTISTROPHE *a c*

Didst thou not start to hear Spain's thrilling pæan
    From land to land re-echoed solemnly,
Till silence became music ?   From the Æan [1]
    To the cold Alps, eternal Italy
      Starts to hear thine !   The sea
Which paves the desert streets of Venice laughs
    In light and music ; widowed Genoa wan,
By moonlight, spells ancestral epitaphs,
    Murmuring, ' Where is Doria ? ' fair Milan,
      Within whose veins long ran
The viper's [2] palsying venom, lifts her heel
To bruise his head.   The signal and the seal
    (If Hope, and Truth, and Justice can avail)
    Art thou of all these hopes.—Oh hail !

ANTISTROPHE *b c*

    Florence, beneath the sun,
    Of cities fairest one,
Blushes within her bower for freedom's expectation :
    From eyes of quenchless hope
    Rome tears the priestly cope,

As ruling once by power, so now by admiration—
    As athlete stripped to run
    From a remoter station
For the high prize lost on Philippi's shore—
As then Hope, Truth, and Justice, did avail,
    So now may Fraud and Wrong ! Oh hail !

EPODE I. *b*

Hear ye the march as of the Earth-born Forms,
    Arrayed against the ever-living gods ?
The crash and darkness of a thousand storms
    Bursting their inaccessible abodes
        Of crags and thunder-clouds ?
See ye the banners blazoned to the day,
    Inwrought with emblems of barbaric pride ?
Dissonant threats kill silence far away ;
    The serene heaven which wraps our Eden wide
        With iron light is dyed.
The Anarchs of the North lead forth their legions,
    Like chaos o'er creation, uncreating ;
An hundred tribes nourished on strange religions
And lawless slaveries. Down the aerial regions
    Of the white Alps, desolating,
    Famished wolves that bide no waiting,
Blotting the glowing footsteps of old glory,
    Trampling our columned cities into dust,
        Their dull and savage lust
    On beauty's corse to sickness satiating—
They come ! The fields they tread look black and hoary
With fire—from their red feet the streams run gory !

EPODE II. *b*

Great Spirit, deepest love,
Which rulest and dost move
All things which live and are within the Italian shore ;
Who spreadest heaven around it,
Whose woods, rocks, waves, surround it ;
Who sittest in thy star, o'er ocean's western floor !
Spirit of Beauty, at whose soft command
The sunbeams and the showers distil its foison
From the earth's bosom chill !
Oh bid those beams be each a blinding brand
Of lightning ! bid those showers be dew of poison !
Bid the earth's plenty kill !
Bid thy bright heaven above,
Whilst light and darkness bound it,
Be their tomb who planned
To make it ours and thine !
Or with thine harmonising ardours fill
And raise thy sons, as o'er the prone horizon
Thy lamp feeds every twilight wave with fire !
Be man's high hope and unextinct desire
The instrument to work thy will divine !
Then clouds from sunbeams, antelopes from leopards,
And frowns and fears from thee,
Would not more swiftly flee
Than Celtic wolves from the Ausonian shepherds.
Whatever, Spirit, from thy starry shrine
Thou yieldest or withholdest, oh let be
The City of thy worship ever free !

25th August 1820.

34

Byron

STANZAS

[While Shelley was writing odes to Liberty and to Naples, Byron at Ravenna was preparing to lead the *carbonari* of the Romagna to battle, and would have done so but for the sudden suppression of the movement in Naples, which eventually led him to die for Greece instead of for Italy. See Introduction, pp. xvii-xviii, above.]

WHEN a man hath no freedom to fight for at home,
　　Let him combat for that of his neighbours ;
Let him think of the glories of Greece and of Rome,
　And get knock'd on the head for his labours.

To do good to mankind is the chivalrous plan
　And is always as nobly requited ;
Then battle for freedom wherever you can,
　And, if not shot or hanged, you 'll get knighted.

Samuel Rogers

ITALY

[Rogers, travelling in Italy in the 'twenties and 'thirties, saw that freedom was stirring, and foretold that Italy would rise again.]

AM I in Italy ?   Is this the Mincius ?
    Are those the distant turrets of Verona ?
And shall I sup where Juliet at the Masque
Saw her loved Montague, and now sleeps by him ?
Such questions hourly do I ask myself ;
And not a stone, in a cross-way, inscribed
' To Mantua '—' to Ferrara '—but excites
Surprise, and doubt, and self-congratulation.
   O Italy, how beautiful thou art !
Yet I could weep—for thou art lying, alas,
Low in the dust ; and we admire thee now
As we admire the beautiful in death.
Thine was a dangerous gift, when thou wast born,
The gift of beauty.   Would thou hadst it not ;
Or wert as once, awing the caitiffs vile
That now beset thee, making thee their slave !
Would they had loved thee less, or feared thee more !
—But why despair ?   Twice hast thou lived already,
Twice shone among the nations of the world,
As the sun shines among the lesser lights
Of heaven ; and shalt again.   The hour shall come,
When they who think to bind the ethereal spirit,

36

SAMUEL ROGERS

Who, like the eagle lowering o'er his prey,
Watch with quick eye, and strike and strike again
If but a sinew vibrate, shall confess
Their wisdom folly.   Even now the flame
Bursts forth where once it burnt so gloriously,
And, dying, left a splendour like the day,
That like the day diffused itself, and still
Blesses the earth,—the light of genius, virtue,
Greatness in thought and act, contempt of death,
God-like example.   Echoes that have slept
Since Athens, Lacedaemon, were Themselves,
Since men invoked ' By those in Marathon ! '
Awake along the Aegean ; and the dead,
They of that sacred shore, have heard the call,
And thro' the ranks, from wing to wing, are seen,
Moving as once they were—instead of rage
Breathing deliberate valour.

Swinburne

SUPER FLUMINA BABYLONIS

[This poem, though written in the 'sixties, admirably describes the moral revival among the educated classes in Italy, under the influence of Mazzini's ethical and political doctrine of Italy a Nation. His propaganda began effectively in 1831 and culminated in 1848. See Introduction, p. xix, above. 'Thee' in the second line means Italy.]

BY the waters of Babylon we sat down and wept,
    Remembering thee,
That for ages of agony hast endured, and slept,
    And wouldst not see.

By the waters of Babylon we stood up and sang,
    Considering thee,
That a blast of deliverance in the darkness rang,
    To set thee free.

And with trumpets and thunderings and with morning song
    Came up the light ;
And thy spirit uplifted thee to forget thy wrong
    As day doth night.

And thy sons were dejected not any more, as then
    When thou wast shamed ;
When thy lovers went heavily without heart, as men
    Whose life was maimed.

SWINBURNE

' On the mountains of memory, by the world's well-springs,
        In all men's eyes,
Where the light of the life of him is on all past things,
        Death only dies.

' Not the light that was quenched for us, nor the deeds
      that were,
        Nor the ancient days,
Nor the sorrows not sorrowful, nor the face most fair
        Of perfect praise.'

So the angel of Italy's resurrection said,
        So yet he saith ;
So the son of her suffering, that from breasts nigh dead
        Drew life, not death.

That the pavement of Golgotha should be white as snow,
        Not red, but white ;
That the waters of Babylon should no longer flow,
        And men see light.

Meredith

MAZZINI

From *Vittoria*, chaps. ii. and xvii.

[See Introduction, p. xx, above.]

HE was a man of middle stature, thin, and even frail, as he stood defined against the sky ; with the complexion of the student, and the student's aspect. The attentive droop of his shoulders and head, the straining of the buttoned coat across his chest, the air as of one who waited and listened, which distinguished his figure, detracted from the promise of other than contemplative energy, until his eyes were fairly seen and felt. That is, until the observer became aware that those soft and large dark meditative eyes had taken hold of him. In them lay no abstracted student's languor, no reflex burning of a solitary lamp ; but a quiet grappling force engaged the penetrating look. Gazing upon them, you were drawn in suddenly among the thousand whirring wheels of a capacious and a vigorous mind, that was both reasoning and prompt, keen of intellect, acting throughout all its machinery, and having all under full command : an orbed mind, supplying its own philosophy, and arriving at the sword-stroke by logical steps,—a mind much less supple than a soldier's ; anything but the mind of a Hamlet. The eyes were dark as the forest's border is dark ; not as night is dark. Under favourable lights their colour was

44

seen to be a deep rich brown, like the chestnut, or more like the hazel-edged sunset brown which lies upon our western rivers in the winter floods, when night begins to shadow them.

The side-view of his face was an expression of classic beauty rarely now to be beheld, either in classic lands or elsewhere. It was severe ; the tender serenity of the full bow of the eyes relieved it. In profile they showed little of their intellectual quality, but what some might have thought a playful luminousness, and some a quick pulse of feeling. The chin was firm ; on it, and on the upper lip, there was a clipped growth of black hair. The whole visage widened upward from the chin, though not very markedly before it reached the broad-lying brows. The temples were strongly indented by the swelling of the forehead above them : and on both sides of the head there ran a pregnant ridge, such as will sometimes lift men a deplorable half inch above the earth we tread. If this man was a problem to others, he was none to himself ; and when others called him an idealist, he accepted the title, reading himself, notwithstanding, as one who was less flighty than many philosophers and professedly practical teachers of his generation. He saw far, and he grasped ends beyond obstacles : he was nourished by sovereign principles ; he despised material present interests ; and, as I have said, he was less supple than a soldier. If the title of idealist belonged to him, we will not immediately decide that it was opprobrious. The idealised conception of stern truths played about his head certainly for those who knew and who loved it. Such a man, perceiving a devout end to be reached, might prove less scrupulous in his course, possibly, and less remorseful, than revolutionary Generals. His smile was quite unclouded, and came softly as a curve in water. It seemed to flow with, and to pass in and out of, his thoughts,—to be a part of his emotion and his meaning when it shone transiently full. For as he had an orbed mind, so had he an orbed nature. The passions were absolutely in harmony with the intelligence. He had the English manner ; a remarkable simplicity contrasting with the demonstrative outcries and gesticulations of his friends when they joined him on the height. Calling them each by name, he received their caresses and took their hands.

*   *   *   *   *   *   *

It was he who preached to the Italians that opportunity is a mocking devil when we look for it to be revealed ; or, in other words, wait for chance ; as it is God's angel when it is created within us, the ripe fruit of virtue and devotion. He cried out to Italians to wait for no inspiration but their own ; that they should never subdue their minds to follow any alien example ; nor let a foreign city of fire be their beacon. Watching over his Italy ; her wrist in his meditative clasp year by year ; he stood like a mystic leech by the couch of a fair and hopeless frame, pledged to revive it by the inspired assurance, shared by none, that life had not forsaken it. A body given over to death and vultures—he stood by it in the desert. Is it a marvel to you that when the carrion-wings swooped low, and the claws fixed, and the beak plucked and savoured its morsel, he raised his arm, and urged the half-resuscitated frame to some vindicating show of existence ? Arise ! he said, even in what appeared most fatal hours of darkness. The slack limbs moved ; the body rose and fell. The cost of the effort was the breaking out of innumerable wounds, old and new ; the gain was the display of the miracle that Italy lived. She tasted her own blood, and herself knew that she lived.

Then she felt her chains. The time was coming for her to prove, by the virtues within her, that she was worthy to live, when others of her sons, subtle and adept, intricate as serpents, bold, unquestioning as well-bestridden steeds, should grapple and play deep for her in the game of worldly strife. Now—at this hour of which I speak—when Austrians marched like a merry flame down Milan streets, and Italians stood like the burnt-out cinders of the fire-grate, Italy's faint wrist was still in the clutch of her grave leech, who counted the beating of her pulse between long pauses, that would have made another think life to be heaving its last, not beginning.

Meredith

MAZZINI'S DOCTRINES

From the Opera of Camilla, *Vittoria*, chap. xxi.

[Any one familiar with Mazzini can see that these are his doctrines, and Meredith indeed tells us so in the words, 'Agostino had done his best to put the heart of the creed of his Chief into these last verses.']

THERE is an end to joy ; there is no end
    To striving ; therefore let us strive
In purity that shall the toil befriend,
And keep our poor mortality alive.

   *   *   *   *   *   *

Our life is but a little holding, lent
To do a mighty labour : we are one
With heaven and the stars when it is spent
To serve God's aim : else die we with the sun.

Meredith

'ITALIA SHALL BE FREE'

[From Vittoria's last song in the Opera, *Vittoria*, chap. xxi.]

I CANNOT count the years
    That you will drink, like me,
The cup of blood and tears,
Ere she to you appears :—
    Italia, Italia, shall be free.

You dedicate your lives
    To her and you will be
The food on which she thrives,
Till her great day arrives :—
    Italia, Italia, shall be free.

She asks you but for faith !
    Your faith in her takes she
As draughts of heaven's breath
Amid defeat and death :—
    Italia, Italia, shall be free.

Robert Browning

THE ITALIAN IN ENGLAND

[This poem was certainly suggested by the life-history and personality of the great exile Mazzini, *par excellence* 'the Italian in England.' The poem (under the title 'Italy in England') appeared in 1845, the year after the affair of the opening of Mazzini's letters by our government which first attracted English public attention to Mazzini's personality. But there are points of unlikeness, and it was not meant for a portrait. Metternich was the reactionary Austrian minister, Italy's greatest enemy until his retirement in 1848.]

THAT second time they hunted me
   From hill to plain, from shore to sea,
And Austria, hounding far and wide
Her blood-hounds thro' the country-side,
Breathed hot and instant on my trace,—
I made six days a hiding-place
Of that dry green old aqueduct
Where I and Charles, when boys, have plucked
The fire-flies from the roof above,
Bright creeping thro' the moss they love:
—How long it seems since Charles was lost!
Six days the soldiers crossed and crossed
The country in my very sight;
And when that peril ceased at night,
The sky broke out in red dismay
With signal fires; well, there I lay
Close covered o'er in my recess,

Up to the neck in ferns and cress,
Thinking on Metternich our friend,
And Charles's miserable end,
And much beside, two days ; the third,
Hunger o'ercame me when I heard
The peasants from the village go
To work among the maize ; you know,
With us in Lombardy, they bring
Provisions packed on mules, a string
With little bells that cheer their task,
And casks, and boughs on every cask
To keep the sun's heat from the wine ;
These I let pass in jingling line,
And, close on them, dear noisy crew,
The peasants from the village, too ;
For at the very rear would troop
Their wives and sisters in a group
To help, I knew.   When these had passed,
I threw my glove to strike the last,
Taking the chance : she did not start,
Much less cry out, but stooped apart,
One instant rapidly glanced round,
And saw me beckon from the ground.
A wild bush grows and hides my crypt ;
She picked my glove up while she stripped
A branch off, then rejoined the rest
With that ; my glove lay in her breast.
Then I drew breath ; they disappeared :
It was for Italy I feared.

An hour, and she returned alone
Exactly where my glove was thrown.

Meanwhile came many thoughts : on me
Rested the hopes of Italy.
I had devised a certain tale
Which, when 'twas told her, could not fail
Persuade a peasant of its truth ;
I meant to call a freak of youth
This hiding, and give hopes of pay,
And no temptation to betray.
But when I saw that woman's face,
Its calm simplicity of grace,
Our Italy's own attitude
In which she walked thus far, and stood,
Planting each naked foot so firm,
To crush the snake and spare the worm—
At first sight of her eyes, I said,
' I am that man upon whose head
' They fix the price, because I hate
' The Austrians over us : the State
' Will give you gold—oh, gold so much !—
' If you betray me to their clutch,
' And be your death, for aught I know,
' If once they find you saved their foe.
' Now, you must bring me food and drink,
' And also paper, pen and ink,
' And carry safe what I shall write
' To Padua, which you 'll reach at night
' Before the duomo shuts ; go in,
' And wait till Tenebræ begin ;
' Walk to the third confessional,
' Between the pillar and the wall,
' And kneeling whisper, *Whence comes peace ?*
' Say it a second time, then cease ;

' And if the voice inside returns,
' *From Christ and Freedom ; what concerns*
' *The cause of Peace ?*—for answer, slip
' My letter where you placed your lip ;
' Then come back happy we have done
' Our mother service—**I**, the son,
' As you the daughter of our land ! '

   Three mornings more, she took her stand
In the same place, with the same eyes :
I was no surer of sun-rise
Than of her coming.   We conferred
Of her own prospects, and I heard
She had a lover—stout and tall,
She said—then let her eyelids fall,
' He could do much '—as if some doubt
Entered her heart,—then, passing out,
' She could not speak for others, who
' Had other thoughts ; herself she knew : '
And so she brought me drink and food.
After four days, the scouts pursued
Another path ; at last arrived
The help my Paduan friends contrived
To furnish me : she brought the news.
For the first time I could not choose
But kiss her hand, and lay my own
Upon her head—' This faith was shown
' To Italy, our mother ; she
' Uses my hand and blesses thee.'
She followed down to the sea-shore ;
I left and never saw her more.

How very long since I have thought
Concerning—much less wished for—aught
Beside the good of Italy,
For which I live and mean to die !
I never was in love ; and since
Charles proved false, what shall now convince
My inmost heart I have a friend ?
However, if I pleased to spend
Real wishes on myself—say, three—
I know at least what one should be.
I would grasp Metternich until
I felt his red wet throat distil
In blood thro' these two hands.   And next,
—Nor much for that am I perplexed—
Charles, perjured traitor, for his part,
Should die slow of a broken heart
Under his new employers.   Last
—Ah, there, what should I wish ?   For fast
Do I grow old and out of strength.
If I resolved to seek at length
My father's house again, how scared
They all would look, and unprepared !
My brothers live in Austria's pay
—Disowned me long ago, men say ;
And all my early mates who used
To praise me so—perhaps induced
More than one early step of mine—
Are turning wise : while some opine
' Freedom grows license,' some suspect
' Haste breeds delay,' and recollect
They always said, such premature
Beginnings never could endure !

So, with a sullen ' All 's for best,'
The land seems settling to its rest.
I think then, I should wish to stand
This evening in that dear, lost land,
Over the sea the thousand miles,
And know if yet that woman smiles
With the calm smile ; some little farm
She lives in there, no doubt : what harm
If I sat on the door-side bench,
And, while her spindle made a trench
Fantastically in the dust,
Inquired of all her fortunes—just
Her children's ages and their names,
And what may be the husband's aims
For each of them.   I 'd talk this out,
And sit there, for an hour about,
Then kiss her hand once more, and lay
Mine on her head, and go my way.

So much for idle wishing—how
It steals the time !   To business now.

Walter Savage Landor

ON THE SLAUGHTER OF THE BROTHERS BANDIERA, BETRAYED TO THE KING OF NAPLES

[In 1844 the two young Venetian nobles, officers in the Austrian navy, suddenly inspired by Mazzini's writings with the conception that Italy was a country, escaped from their ships, and with a handful of companions invaded the Neapolitan kingdom to dethrone the Bourbons and establish the régime of liberty among their brethren of the South. They and their companions were shot near Cosenza, and the story of their hopeless self-devotion took a high place in the Italian martyrology.]

BORNE on white horses, which the God of Thrace
 Rein'd not for wanton glory in the race
  Of Elis, when from far
  Ran forth the regal car,
Even from Syracuse, across the sea,
To roll its thunder thro' that fruitless lea ;
  No ; but on steeds whose foam
  Flew o'er the helm of Rome,
Came Castor and his brother ; at which sight
A shout of victory drown'd the din of fight.
  O Rome ! O Italy !
  Doom'd are ye, doom'd to see
Nor guides divine nor high-aspiring men,
Nor proudly tread the battlefield again ?
  Lo ! who are they who land
  Upon that southern strand ?

ELIZABETH BARRETT BROWNING

From older singers' lips who sang not thus
    Exultingly and purely, yet, with pang
Fast sheathed in music, touched the heart of us
    So finely that the pity scarcely pained.
I thought how Filicaja [1] led on others,
    Bewailers for their Italy enchained,
And how they called her childless among mothers,
    Widow of empires, ay, and scarce refrained
Cursing her beauty to her face, as brothers
    Might a shamed sister's,—' Had she been less fair
She were less wretched ; '—how, evoking so
    From congregated wrong and heaped despair
Of men and women writhing under blow,
    Harrowed and hideous in a filthy lair,
Some personating Image wherein woe
    Was wrapt in beauty from offending much,
They called it Cybele, or Niobe,
    Or laid it corpse-like on a bier for such,
Where all the world might drop for Italy
    Those cadenced tears which burn not where they touch,—
' Juliet of nations, canst thou die as we ?
    And was the violet crown that crowned thy head
So over-large, though new buds made it rough,
    It slipped down and across thine eyelids dead,
O sweet, fair Juliet ? ' Of such songs enough,
    Too many of such complaints ! behold, instead,
Void at Verona, Juliet's marble trough ! *
    As void as that is, are all images

* They show at Verona, as the tomb of Juliet, an empty trough or stone.

63

Men set between themselves and actual wrong,
  To catch the weight of pity, meet the stress
Of conscience,—since 'tis easier to gaze long
  On mournful masks and sad effigies
Than on real, live, weak creatures crushed by strong.

  For me who stand in Italy to-day
Where worthier poets stood and sang before,
  I kiss their footsteps yet their words gainsay.
I can but muse in hope upon this shore
  Of golden Arno as it shoots away
Through Florence' heart beneath her bridges four :
  Bent bridges, seeming to strain off like bows,
And tremble while the arrowy undertide
  Shoots on and cleaves the marble as it goes,
And strikes up palace-walls on either side,
  And froths the cornice out in glittering rows,
With doors and windows quaintly multiplied,
  And terrace-sweeps, and gazers upon all,
By whom if flower or kerchief were thrown out
  From any lattice there, the same would fall
Into the river underneath, no doubt,
  It runs so close and fast 'twixt wall and wall.
How beautiful ! the mountains from without
  In silence listen for the word said next.
What word will men say,—here where Giotto planted
  His campanile like an unperplexed
Fine question Heaven-ward, touching the things
    granted
  A noble people who, being greatly vexed
In act, in aspiration keep undaunted ?
  What word will God say ?   Michel's Night and Day

And Dawn and Twilight wait in marble scorn *
  Like dogs upon a dunghill, couched on clay
From whence the Medicean stamp 's outworn,
  The final putting off of all such sway
By all such hands, and freeing of the unborn
  In Florence and the great world outside Florence.
Three hundred years his patient statues wait
  In that small chapel of the dim Saint Lawrence :
Day's eyes are breaking bold and passionate
  Over his shoulder, and will flash abhorrence
On darkness and with level looks meet fate,
  When once loose from that marble film of theirs ;
The Night has wild dreams in her sleep, the Dawn
  Is haggard as the sleepless, Twilight wears
A sort of horror ; as the veil withdrawn
  'Twixt the artist's soul and works had left them heirs
Of speechless thoughts which would not quail nor fawn,
  Of angers and contempts, of hope and love :
For not without a meaning did he place
  The princely Urbino on the seat above
With everlasting shadow on his face,
  While the slow dawns and twilights disapprove
The ashes of his long-extinguished race.

   *   *   *   *   *   *   *

' Less wretched if less fair.'   Perhaps a truth
Is so far plain in this, that Italy,
  Long trammelled with the purple of her youth
Against her age's ripe activity,
  Sits still upon her tombs, without death's ruth

---

  * These famous statues recline in the Sagrestia Nuova, on the
tombs of Giuliano de' Medici, third son of Lorenzo the Magnificent,
and Lorenzo of Urbino, his grandson.

E   65

But also without life's brave energy.
 ' Now tell us what is Italy ? ' men ask :
And others answer, ' Virgil, Cicero,
 Catullus, Cæsar.' What beside ? to task
The memory closer—' Why, Boccaccio,
 Dante, Petrarca,'—and if still the flask
Appears to yield its wine by drops too slow,—
 ' Angelo, Raffael, Pergolese,'—all
Whose strong hearts beat through stone, or charged
  again
 The paints with fire of souls electrical,
Or broke up heaven for music. What more then ?
 Why, then, no more. The chaplet's last beads fall
In naming the last saintship within ken,
 And, after that, none prayeth in the land.
Alas, this Italy has too long swept
 Heroic ashes up for hour-glass sand ;
Of her own past, impassioned nympholept !
* * * * * * *

 We do not serve the dead—the past is past.
God lives, and lifts His glorious mornings up
 Before the eyes of men awake at last,
Who put away the meats they used to sup,
 And down upon the dust of earth outcast
The dregs remaining of the ancient cup,
 Then turn to wakeful prayer and worthy act.
The Dead, upon their awful 'vantage ground,
 The sun not in their faces, shall abstract
No more our strength ; we will not be discrowned
 As guardians of their crowns, nor deign transact
A barter of the present, for a sound
 Of good so counted in the foregone days.

ELIZABETH BARRETT BROWNING

O Dead, ye shall no longer cling to us
　　With rigid hands of desiccating praise,
And drag us backward by the garment thus,
　　To stand and laud you in long-drawn virelays !
We will not henceforth be oblivious
　　Of our own lives, because ye lived before,
Nor of our acts, because ye acted well.
　　We thank you that ye first unlatched the door,
But will not make it inaccessible
　　By thankings on the threshold any more.
We hurry onward to extinguish hell
　　With our fresh souls, our younger hope, and God's
Maturity of purpose.　　Soon shall we
　　Die also !　and, that then our periods
Of life may round themselves to memory
　　As smoothly as on our graves the burial-sods,
We now must look to it to excel as ye,
　　And bear our age as far, unlimited
By the last mind-mark ; so, to be invoked
　　By future generations, as their Dead.

'Tis true that when the dust of death has choked
　　A great man's voice, the common words he said
Turn oracles, the common thoughts he yoked
　　Like horses, draw like griffins : this is true
And acceptable.　I, too, should desire,
　　When men make record, with the flowers they strew,
' Savonarola's soul went out in fire
　　Upon our Grand-duke's piazza,* and burned through

* Savonarola was burnt for his testimony against papal corruptions as early as March 1498 ; and, as late as our own day, it has been a custom in Florence to strew with violets the pavement where he suffered, in grateful recognition of the anniversary.

A moment first, or ere he did expire,
    The veil betwixt the right and wrong, and showed
How near God sate and judged the judges there,—'
    Upon the self-same pavement overstrewed
To cast my violets with as reverent care,
    And prove that all the winters which have snowed
Cannot snow out the scent from stones and air,
    Of a sincere man's virtues.   This was he,
Savonarola, who, while Peter sank
    With his whole boat-load, called courageously
' Wake Christ, wake Christ ! '—who, having tried the tank
    Of old church-waters used for baptistry
Ere Luther came to spill them, swore they stank ;
    Who also by a princely deathbed cried,
' Loose Florence, or God will not loose thy soul ! ' [2]
    Then fell back the Magnificent and died
Beneath the star-look shooting from the cowl,
    Which turned to wormwood-bitterness the wide
Deep sea of his ambitions.   It were foul
    To grudge Savonarola and the rest
Their violets : rather pay them quick and fresh !
    The emphasis of death makes manifest
The eloquence of action in our flesh ;
    And men who, living, were but dimly guessed,
When once free from their life's entangled mesh,
    Show their full length in graves, or oft indeed
Exaggerate their stature, in the flat,
    To noble admirations which exceed
Most nobly, yet will calculate in that
    But accurately.   We, who are the seed
Of buried creatures, if we turned and spat
    Upon our antecedents, we were vile.

Bring violets rather.   If these had not walked
  Their furlong, could we hope to walk our mile ?
Therefore bring violets.   Yet if we self-baulked
  Stand still, a-strewing violets all the while,
These moved in vain, of whom we have vainly talked.
  So rise up henceforth with a cheerful smile,
And having strewn the violets, reap the corn,
  And having reaped and garnered, bring the plough
And draw new furrows 'neath the healthy morn,
  And plant the great Hereafter in this Now.

    *   *   *   *   *   *   *

                Shall I say
What made my heart beat with exulting love
A few weeks back ?—
                The day was such a day,
  As Florence owes the sun.   The sky above,
Its weight upon the mountains seemed to lay
  And palpitate in glory, like a dove
Who has flown too fast, full-hearted—take away
  The image ! for the heart of man beat higher
That day in Florence, flooding all her streets
  And piazzas with a tumult and desire.
The people, with accumulated heats
  And faces turned one way, as if one fire
Both drew and flushed them, left their ancient beats
  And went up toward the palace-Pitti wall
To thank their Grand-duke who, not quite of course,
  Had graciously permitted, at their call,
The citizens to use their civic force
  To guard their civic homes.[3] So, one and all,
The Tuscan cities streamed up to the source
  Of this new good at Florence, taking it

As good so far, presageful of more good,—
    The first torch of Italian freedom, lit
To toss in the next tiger's face who should
    Approach too near them in a greedy fit—
The first pulse of an even flow of blood
    To prove the level of Italian veins
Towards rights perceived and granted.   How we gazed
    From Casa Guidi windows while, in trains
Of orderly procession—banners raised,
    And intermittent bursts of martial strains
Which died upon the shout as if amazed,
    By gladness beyond music—they passed on !
The Magistracy, with insignia, passed,—
    And all the people shouted in the sun,
And all the thousand windows which had cast
    A ripple of silks in blue and scarlet down
(As if the houses overflowed at last),
    Seemed growing larger with fair heads and eyes.
The Lawyers passed,—and still arose the shout,
    And hands broke from the windows to surprise
Those grave calm brows with bay-tree leaves thrown out.
    The Priesthood passed,—the friars with worldly-wise
Keen sidelong glances from their beards about
    The street to see who shouted ; many a monk
Who takes a long rope in the waist, was there :
    Whereat the popular exultation drunk
With indrawn ' vivas ' the whole sunny air,
    While through the murmuring windows rose and sunk
A cloud of kerchiefed hands,—' The church makes fair
    Her welcome in the new Pope's name.'   Ensued
The black sign of the ' Martyrs '—(name no name,
    But count the graves in silence).   Next were viewed

The Artists ; next, the Trades ; and after came
   The People,—flag and sign, and rights as good—
And very loud the shout was for that same
   Motto, ' Il popolo.' IL POPOLO,—
The word means dukedom, empire, majesty,
   And kings in such an hour might read it so.
And next, with banners, each in his degree,
   Deputed representatives a-row
Of every separate state of Tuscany :
   Siena's she-wolf, bristling on the fold
Of the first flag, preceded Pisa's hare,
   And Massa's lion floated calm in gold,
Pienza's following with his silver stare,
   Arezzo's steed pranced clear from bridle-hold,—
And well might shout our Florence, greeting there
   These, and more brethren.   Last, the world had sent
The various children of her teeming flanks—
   Greeks, English, French—as if to a parliament
Of lovers of her Italy in ranks,
   Each bearing its land's symbol reverent ;
At which the stones seemed breaking into thanks
   And rattling up the sky, such sounds in proof
Arose ; the very house-walls seemed to bend ;
   The very windows, up from door to roof,
Flashed out a rapture of bright heads, to mend
   With passionate looks the gesture's whirling off
A hurricane of leaves.   Three hours did end
   While all these passed ; and ever in the crowd,
Rude men, unconscious of the tears that kept
   Their beards moist, shouted ; some few laughed aloud,
And none asked any why they laughed and wept :
   Friends kissed each other's cheeks, and foes long vowed

More warmly did it ; two-months' babies leapt
    Right upward in their mothers' arms, whose black
Wide glittering eyes looked elsewhere ; lovers pressed
    Each before either, neither glancing back ;
And peasant maidens smoothly 'tired and tressed
    Forgot to finger on their throats the slack
Great pearl-strings ; while old blind men would not rest,
    But pattered with their staves and slid their shoes
Along the stones, and smiled as if they saw.
    O heaven, I think that day had noble use
Among God's days ! So near stood Right and Law,
    Both mutually forborne ! Law would not bruise,
Nor Right deny, and each in reverent awe
    Honoured the other. And if, ne'ertheless
That good day's sun delivered to the vines
    No charta, and the liberal Duke's excess
Did scarce exceed a Guelf's or Ghibelline's
    In any special actual righteousness
Of what that day he granted, still the signs
    Are good and full of promise, we must say,
When multitudes approach their kings with prayers
    And kings concede their people's right to pray,
Both in one sunshine. Griefs are not despairs,
    So uttered, nor can royal claims dismay
When men from humble homes and ducal chairs,
    Hate wrong together. It was well to view
Those banners ruffled in a ruler's face
    Inscribed, ' Live freedom, union, and all true
Brave patriots who are aided by God's grace ! '
    Nor was it ill when Leopoldo drew
His little children to the window-place
    He stood in at the Pitti, to suggest

ELIZABETH BARRETT BROWNING

We pass these things,—because ' the times ' are prest
   With necessary charges of the weight
Of all this sin, and ' Calvin, for the rest,
   Made bold to burn Servetus.   Ah, men err ! '—
And so do *churches* ! which is all we mean
   To bring to proof in any register
Of theological fat kine and lean :
   So drive them back into the pens ! refer
Old sins (with pourpoint, ' quotha ' and ' I ween ')
   Entirely to the old times, the old times ;
Nor ever ask why this preponderant
   Infallible pure Church could set her chimes
Most loudly then, just then,—most jubilant,
   Precisely then, when mankind stood in crimes
Full heart-deep, and Heaven's judgments were not scant.
   Inquire still less, what signifies a church
Of perfect inspiration and pure laws
   Who burns the first man with a brimstone-torch,
And grinds the second, bone by bone, because
   The times, forsooth, are used to rack and scorch !
What *is* a holy Church unless she awes
   The times down from their sins ?   Did Christ select
Such amiable times, to come and teach
   Love to, and mercy ?   The whole world were wrecked
If every mere great man, who lives to reach
   A little leaf of popular respect,
Attained not simply by some special breach
   In the age's customs, by some precedence
In thought and act, which, having proved him higher
   Than those he lived with, proved his competence
In helping them to wonder and aspire.

   *   *   *   *   *   *   *

To leave which lures
Of wider subject through past years,—behold,
We come back from the popedom to the pope,
To ponder what he *must* be, ere we are bold
For what he *may* be, with our heavy hope
To trust upon his soul.   So, fold by fold,
Explore this mummy in the priestly cope,
Transmitted through the darks of time, to catch
The man within the wrappage, and discern
How he, an honest man, upon the watch
Full fifty years for what a man may learn,
Contrived to get just there ; with what a snatch
Of old-world oboli he had to earn
The passage through ; with what a drowsy sop,
To drench the busy barkings of his brain ;
What ghosts of pale tradition, wreathed with hope
'Gainst wakeful thought, he had to entertain
For heavenly visions ; and consent to stop
The clock at noon, and let the hour remain
(Without vain windings-up) inviolate
Against all chimings from the belfry.   Lo,
From every given pope you must abate,
Albeit you love him, some things—good, you know—
Which every given heretic you hate,
Assumes for his, as being plainly so.
A pope must hold by popes a little,—yes,
By councils, from Nicæa up to Trent,—
By hierocratic empire, more or less
Irresponsible to men,—he must resent
Each man's particular conscience, and repress
Inquiry, meditation, argument,
As tyrants faction.   Also, he must not

76

Love truth too dangerously, but prefer
  ' The interests of the Church ' (because a blot
Is better than a rent, in miniver)—
  Submit to see the people swallow hot
Husk-porridge, which his chartered churchmen stir
  Quoting the only true God's epigraph,
' Feed my lambs, Peter ! '—must consent to sit
  Attesting with his pastoral ring and staff
To such a picture of our Lady, hit
  Off well by artist-angels (though not half
As fair as Giotto would have painted it)—
  To such a vial, where a dead man's blood
Runs yearly warm beneath a churchman's finger,—
  To such a holy house of stone and wood,
Whereof a cloud of angels was the bringer
  From Bethlehem to Loreto. Were it good
For any pope on earth to be a flinger
  Of stones against these high-niched counterfeits ?
Apostates only are iconoclasts.
  He dares not say, while this false thing abets
That true thing, ' This is false.' He keeps his fasts
  And prayers, as prayer and fast were silver frets
To change a note upon a string that lasts,
  And make a lie a virtue. Now, if he
Did more than this, higher hoped, and braver dared,
  I think he were a pope in jeopardy,
Or no pope rather, for his truth had barred
  The vaulting of his life,—and certainly,
If he do only this, mankind's regard
  Moves on from him at once, to seek some new
Teacher and leader. He is good and great
  According to the deeds a pope can do ;

Most liberal, save those bonds ; affectionate,
    As princes may be, and, as priests are, true ;
But only the ninth Pius after eight,
    When all 's praised most.   At best and hopefullest,
He 's pope—we want a man ! his heart beats
    warm,
    But, like the prince enchanted to the waist,
He sits in stone and hardens by a charm
    Into the marble of his throne high-placed.
Mild benediction waves his saintly arm—
    So, good ! but what we want 's a perfect man,
Complete and all alive : half travertine
    Half suits our need, and ill subserves our plan.
Feet, knees, nerves, sinews, energies divine
    Were never yet too much for men who ran
In such hard ways as must be this of thine,
    Deliverer whom we seek, whoe'er thou art,
Pope, prince, or peasant !   If, indeed, the first,
    The noblest, therefore ! since the heroic heart
Within thee must be great enough to burst
    Those trammels buckling to the baser part
Thy saintly peers in Rome, who crossed and cursed
    With the same finger.

     *   *   *   *   *   *   *

Meanwhile, let all the far ends of the world
    Breathe back the deep breath of their old delight,
To swell the Italian banner just unfurled.
    Help, lands of Europe ! for, if Austria fight,
The drums will bar your slumber.   Had ye curled
    The laurel for your thousand artists' brows,
If these Italian hands had planted none ?
    Can any sit down idle in the house

Nor hear appeals from Buonarroti's stone
  And Raffael's canvas, rousing and to rouse ?
*   *   *   *   *   *   *
And Vallombrosa, we two went to see
  Last June, beloved companion,—where sublime
The mountains live in holy families,
  And the slow pinewoods ever climb and climb
Half up their breasts, just stagger as they seize
  Some grey crag, drop back with it many a time,
And straggle blindly down the precipice.
  The Vallombrosan brooks were strewn as thick
That June-day, knee-deep with dead beechen leaves
  As Milton saw them ere his heart grew sick
And his eyes blind.   I think the monks and beeves
  Are all the same too ; scarce have they changed the
    wick
On good St. Gualbert's altar which receives
  The convent's pilgrims ; and the pool in front
(Wherein the hill-stream trout are cast, to wait
  The beatific vision and the grunt
Used at refectory) keeps its weedy state,
  To baffle saintly abbots who would count
The fish across their breviary nor 'bate
  The measure of their steps.   O waterfalls
And forests ! sound and silence ! mountains bare
  That leap up peak by peak and catch the palls
Of purple and silver mist to rend and share
  With one another, at electric calls
Of life in the sunbeams,—till we cannot dare
  Fix your shapes, count your number ! we must think
Your beauty and your glory helped to fill
  The cup of Milton's soul so to the brink,

He never more was thirsty when God's will
   Had shattered to his sense the last chain-link
By which he had drawn from Nature's visible
   The fresh well-water. Satisfied by this,
He sang of Adam's paradise and smiled,
   Remembering Vallombrosa. Therefore is
The place divine to English man and child,
   And pilgrims leave their souls here in a kiss.

For Italy 's the whole earth's treasury piled,
   With reveries of gentle ladies, flung
Aside, like ravelled silk, from life's worn stuff ;
   With coins of scholars' fancy, which, being rung
On work-day counter, still sound silver-proof ;
   In short, with all the dreams of dreamers young,
Before their heads have time for slipping off
   Hope's pillow to the ground. How oft, indeed,
We 've sent our souls out from the rigid north,
   On bare white feet which would not print nor bleed,
To climb the Alpine passes and look forth,
   Where booming low the Lombard rivers lead
To gardens, vineyards, all a dream is worth,
   Sights, thou and I, Love, have seen afterward
From Tuscan Bellosguardo, wide awake,*
   When, standing on the actual blessed sward
Where Galileo stood at nights to take
   The vision of the stars, we have found it hard,
Gazing upon the earth and heaven, to make
   A choice of beauty.

* Galileo's villa, close to Florence, is built on an eminence called
Bellosguardo.

ELIZABETH BARRETT BROWNING

Therefore let us all
Refreshed in England or in other land,
  By visions, with their fountain-rise and fall,
Of this earth's darling,—we, who understand
  A little how the Tuscan musical
Vowels do round themselves as if they planned
  Eternities of separate sweetness,—we,
Who loved Sorrento vines in picture-book,
  Or ere in wine-cup we pledged faith or glee,—
Who loved Rome's wolf with demi-gods at suck,
  Or ere we loved truth's own divinity,—
Who loved, in brief, the classic hill and brook,
  And Ovid's dreaming tales and Petrarch's song,
Or ere we loved Love's self even,—let us give
  The blessing of our souls (and wish them strong
To bear it to the height where prayers arrive,
  When faithful spirits pray against a wrong)
To this great cause of southern men who strive
  In God's name for man's rights, and shall not
    fail!

Behold, they shall not fail. The shouts ascend
  Above the shrieks, in Naples, and prevail.
Rows of shot corpses, waiting for the end
  Of burial, seem to smile up straight and pale
Into the azure air and apprehend
  That final gun-flash from Palermo's coast
Which lightens their apocalypse of death.[8]
  So let them die! The world shows nothing lost;
Therefore, not blood. Above or underneath,
  What matter, brothers, if ye keep your post
On duty's side? As sword returns to sheath,

F   81

So dust to grave, but souls find place in Heaven.
Heroic daring is the true success,
    The eucharistic bread requires no leaven ;
And though your ends were hopeless, we should bless
    Your cause as holy.   Strive—and, having striven,
Take, for God's recompense, that righteousness !

CASA GUIDI WINDOWS

PART II

[Written in 1851 after the failure of the hopes of Italy, and the ignominious collapse of the Tuscan revolution in 1849. The peaceable Tuscans, whose conduct the Brownings witnessed from their windows, had shown less fight than the North Italians, Romagnoles, or Sicilians.]

I WROTE a meditation and a dream,
    Hearing a little child sing in the street :
I leant upon his music as a theme,
    Till it gave way beneath my heart's full beat
Which tried at an exultant prophecy
    But dropped before the measure was complete—
Alas, for songs and hearts !   O Tuscany,
    O, Dante's Florence, is the type too plain ?
Didst thou, too, only sing of liberty
    As little children take up a high strain
With unintentioned voices, and break off
    To sleep upon their mother's knees again ?
Couldst thou not watch one hour ? then, sleep enough—
    That sleep may hasten manhood and sustain
The faint pale spirit with some muscular stuff.

    *   *   *   *   *   *   *

From Casa Guidi windows I looked forth,
And saw ten thousand eyes of Florentines
    Flash back the triumph of the Lombard north,—
Saw fifty banners, freighted with the signs
    And exultations of the awakened earth,
Float on above the multitude in lines,
    Straight to the Pitti.   So, the vision went,
And so, between those populous rough hands
    Raised in the sun, Duke Leopold outleant,
And   took   the   patriot's   oath   which   henceforth
        stands
    Among the oaths of perjurers, eminent
To catch the lightnings ripened for these lands.

*   *   *   *   *   *   *

From Casa Guidi windows I looked out,
Again looked, and beheld a different sight.
    The Duke had fled before the people's shout
' Long live the Duke ! '   A people, to speak right,
    Must speak as soft as courtiers, lest a doubt
Should curdle brows of gracious sovereigns, white.
    Moreover that same dangerous shouting meant
Some gratitude for future favours, which
    Were only promised, the Constituent
Implied, the whole being subject to the hitch
    In ' motu proprios,' very incident
To all these Czars, from Paul to Paulovitch.
    Whereat the people rose up in the dust
Of the ruler's flying feet, and shouted still
    And loudly ; only, this time, as was just,
Not ' Live the Duke,' who had fled for good or ill,
    But ' Live the People,' who remained and must,
The unrenounced and unrenounceable.

Long live the people ! How they lived ! and boiled
And bubbled in the cauldron of the street :
　　How the young blustered, nor the old recoiled,
And what a thunderous stir of tongues and feet
　　Trod flat the palpitating bells and foiled
The joy-guns of their echo, shattering it !
　　How down they pulled the Duke's arms everywhere !
How up they set new café-signs, to show
　　Where patriots might sip ices in pure air—
(The fresh paint smelling somewhat) ! To and fro
　　How marched the civic guard, and stopped to stare
When boys broke windows in a civic glow !
　　How rebel songs were sung to loyal tunes,
And bishops cursed in ecclesiastic metres :
　　How all the Circoli [1] grew large as moons,
And all the speakers, moonstruck,—thankful greeters
　　Of prospects which struck poor the ducal boons,
A mere free Press, and Chambers !—frank repeaters
　　Of great Guerazzi's [2] praises—' There 's a man,
The father of the land, who, truly great,
　　Takes off that national disgrace and ban,
The farthing tax upon our Florence-gate,
　　And saves Italia as he only can ! '
How all the nobles fled, and would not wait,
　　Because they were most noble,—which being so,
How liberals vowed to burn their palaces,
　　Because free Tuscans were not free to go !
How grown men raged at Austria's wickedness,
　　And smoked,—while fifty striplings in a row
Marched straight to Piedmont for the wrong's redress ! [3]
　　You say we failed in duty, we who wore
Black velvet like Italian democrats,

Who slashed our sleeves like patriots, nor forswore
The true republic in the form of hats ?
We chased the archbishop from the Duomo-door,
We chalked the walls with bloody caveats
   Against all tyrants. If we did not fight
Exactly, we fired muskets up the air
   To show that victory was ours of right.
We met, had free discussion everywhere
   (Except perhaps i' the Chambers) day and night.
We proved the poor should be employed, . . . that's fair,—
   And yet the rich not worked for anywise,—
Pay certified, yet payers abrogated,—
   Full work secured, yet liabilities
To overwork excluded,—not one bated
   Of all our holidays, that still, at twice
Or thrice a week, are moderately rated.
   We proved that Austria was dislodged, or would
Or should be, and that Tuscany in arms
   Should, would dislodge her, ending the old feud ;
And yet, to leave our piazzas, shops, and farms,
   For the simple sake of fighting, was not good—
We proved that also.
     *   *   *   *   *   *   *
Conviction was not, courage failed, and truth
   Was something to be doubted of. The mime
Changed masks, because a mime. The tide as smooth
   In running in as out, no sense of crime
Because no sense of virtue,—sudden ruth
   Seized on the people : they would have again
Their good Grand-duke and leave Guerazzi, though
   He took that tax from Florence. ' Much in vain
He takes it from the market-carts, we trow,

While urgent that no market-men remain,
But all march off and leave the spade and plough,
　　To die among the Lombards.[4]　Was it thus
The dear paternal Duke did ?　Live the Duke ! '
　　At which the joy-bells multitudinous,
Swept by an opposite wind, as loudly shook.
　　Call back the mild archbishop to his house,
To bless the people with his frightened look,—
　　He shall not yet be hanged, you comprehend !
Seize on Guerazzi ; guard him in full view,
　　Or else we stab him in the back, to end !
Rub out those chalked devices, set up new
　　The Duke's arms, doff your Phrygian caps, and mend
The pavement of the piazzas broke into
　　By barren poles of freedom : smooth the way
For the ducal carriage, lest his highness sigh
　　' Here trees of liberty grew yesterday ! '
' Long live the Duke ! '—how roared the cannonry,
　　How rocked the bell-towers, and through thickening
　　　spray
Of nosegays, wreaths, and kerchiefs tossed on high,
　　How marched the civic guard, the people still
Being good at shouts, especially the boys !
　　Alas, poor people, of an unfledged will
Most fitly expressed by such a callow voice !
　　Alas, still poorer Duke, incapable
Of being worthy even of so much noise !

You think he came back instantly, with thanks
And tears in his faint eyes, and hands extended
　　To stretch the franchise through their utmost ranks ?
That having, like a father, apprehended,
86

He came to pardon fatherly those pranks
Played out and now in filial service ended ?—
   That some love-token, like a prince, he threw
To meet the people's love-call, in return ?
   Well, how he came I will relate to you ;
And if your hearts should burn, why, hearts *must* burn,
   To make the ashes which things old and new
Shall be washed clean in—as this Duke will learn.[5]

   From Casa Guidi windows gazing, then,
I saw and witness how the Duke came back.
   The regular tramp of horse and tread of men
Did smite the silence like an anvil black
   And sparkless.   With her wide eyes at full strain,
Our Tuscan nurse exclaimed, ' Alack, alack,
   Signora ! these shall be the Austrians.'   ' Nay,
Be still,' I answered, ' do not wake the child ! '
   —For so, my two-months' baby sleeping lay
In milky dreams upon the bed and smiled,
   And I thought, ' He shall sleep on, while he may,
Through the world's baseness : not being yet defiled,
   Why should he be disturbed by what is done ? '
Then, gazing, I beheld the long-drawn street
   Live out, from end to end, full in the sun,
With Austria's thousand ; sword and bayonet,
   Horse, foot, artillery,—cannons rolling on
Like blind slow storm-clouds gestant with the heat
   Of undeveloped lightnings, each bestrode
By a single man, dust-white from head to heel,
   Indifferent as the dreadful thing he rode,
Like a sculptured Fate serene and terrible.
   As some smooth river which has overflowed,

Will slow and silent down its current wheel
    A loosened forest, all the pines erect,
So swept, in mute significance of storm,
    The marshalled thousands; not an eye deflect
To left or right, to catch a novel form
    Of Florence city adorned by architect
And carver, or of Beauties live and warm
    Scared at the casements,—all, straightforward eyes
And faces, held as steadfast as their swords,
    And cognisant of acts, not imageries.
The key, O Tuscans, too well fits the wards!
    Ye asked for mimes,—these bring you tragedies:
For purple,—these shall wear it as your lords.
    Ye played like children,—die like innocents.
Ye mimicked lightnings with a torch,—the crack
    Of the actual bolt, your pastime circumvents.
Ye called up ghosts, believing they were slack
    To follow any voice from Gilboa's tents, . . .
Here 's Samuel!—and, so, Grand-dukes come back!
    *   *   *   *   *   *   *

    Meanwhile, from Casa Guidi windows, we
Beheld the armament of Austria flow
    Into the drowning heart of Tuscany:
And yet none wept, none cursed, or, if 'twas so,
    They wept and cursed in silence.   Silently
Our noisy Tuscans watched the invading foe;
    They had learnt silence.   Pressed against the wall,
And grouped upon the church-steps opposite,
    A few pale men and women stared at all.
God knows what they were feeling, with their white
    Constrainèd faces, they, so prodigal
Of cry and gesture when the world goes right,

Or wrong indeed.   But here was depth of wrong,
And here, still water; they were silent here;
   And through that sentient silence, struck along
That measured tramp from which it stood out clear,
   Distinct the sound and silence, like a gong
At midnight, each by the other awfuller,—
   While every soldier in his cap displayed
A leaf of olive.   Dusty, bitter thing!
   Was such plucked at Novara, is it said? [6]

   *   *   *   *   *   *   *

But wherefore should we look out any more
   From Casa Guidi windows?   Shut them straight,
And let us sit down by the folded door,
   And veil our saddened faces and, so, wait
What next the judgment-heavens make ready for.
   I have grown too weary of these windows.   Sights
Come thick enough and clear enough in thought,
   Without the sunshine; souls have inner lights.
And since the Grand-duke has come back and brought
   This army of the North which thus requites
His filial South, we leave him to be taught.
   His South, too, has learnt something certainly,
Whereof the practice will bring profit soon;
   And peradventure other eyes may see,
From Casa Guidi windows, what is done
   Or undone.   Whatsoever deeds they be,
Pope Pius will be glorified in none.

   Record that gain, Mazzini!—it shall top
Some heights of sorrow.   Peter's rock, so named,
   Shall lure no vessel any more to drop
Among the breakers.[7]   Peter's chair is shamed

Like any vulgar throne the nations lop
To pieces for their firewood unreclaimed,—
And, when it burns too, we shall see as well
In Italy as elsewhere.   Let it burn.
The cross, accounted still adorable,
Is Christ's cross only !—if the thief's would earn
Some stealthy genuflexions, we rebel ;
And here the impenitent thief's has had its turn,
As God knows ; and the people on their knees
Scoff and toss back the crosiers stretched like yokes
To press their heads down lower by degrees.
So Italy, by means of these last strokes,
Escapes the danger which preceded these,
Of leaving captured hands in cloven oaks,—
Of leaving very souls within the buckle
Whence bodies struggled outward,—of supposing
That freemen may like bondsmen kneel and truckle
And then stand up as usual, without losing
An inch of stature.

   *   *   *   *   *   *   *

Why, almost, through this Pius, we believed
The priesthood could be an honest thing, he smiled
So saintly while our corn was being sheaved
For his own granaries ! Showing now defiled
His hireling hands, a better help 's achieved
Than if they blessed us shepherd-like and mild.
False doctrine, strangled by its own amen,
Dies in the throat of all this nation.   Who
Will speak a pope's name as they rise again ?
What woman or what child will count him true ?
What dreamer, praise him with the voice or pen ?
What man, fight for him ?—Pius takes his due.

ELIZABETH BARRETT BROWNING

Of the gorgeous Crystal Palace. Every nation,
  To every other nation strange of yore,
Gives face to face the civic salutation,
  And holds up in a proud right hand before
That congress the best work which she can fashion
  By her best means.

*   *   *   *   *   *   *

  O Magi of the east and of the west,
Your incense, gold and myrrh are excellent !—
  What gifts for Christ, then, bring ye with the rest ?
Your hands have worked well : is your courage
      spent
  In handwork only ?   Have you nothing best,
Which generous souls may perfect and present,
  And He shall thank the givers for ? no light
Of teaching, liberal nations, for the poor
  Who sit in darkness when it is not night ?
No cure for wicked children ?   Christ,—no cure !
  No help for women sobbing out of sight
Because men made the laws ? no brothel lure
  Burnt out by popular lightnings ?   Hast thou found
No remedy, my England, for such woes ?
  No outlet, Austria, for the scourged and bound,
No entrance for the exiled ? no repose,
  Russia, for knouted Poles worked underground,
And gentle ladies bleached among the snows ?
  No mercy for the slave, America ?
No hope for Rome, free France, chivalric France ?
  Alas, great nations have great shames, I say.
No pity, O world, no tender utterance
  Of benediction, and prayers stretched this way
For poor Italia, baffled by mischance ?

O gracious nations, give some ear to me !
You all go to your Fair, and I am one
  Who at the roadside of humanity
Beseech your alms,—God's justice to be done.
  So, prosper !
             In the name of Italy,
Meantime, her patriot Dead have benison.
  They only have done well ; and, what they did
Being perfect, it shall triumph.   Let them slumber :
  No king of Egypt in a pyramid
Is safer from oblivion, though he number
  Full seventy cerements for a coverlid.
These Dead be seeds of life, and shall encumber
  The sad heart of the land until it loose
The clammy clods and let out the Spring-growth
  In beatific green through every bruise.
The tyrant should take heed to what he doth,
  Since every victim-carrion turns to use,
And drives a chariot, like a god made wroth,
  Against each piled injustice.   Ay, the least,
Dead for Italia, not in vain has died ;
  Though many vainly, ere life's struggle ceased,
To mad dissimilar ends have swerved aside ;
  Each grave her nationality has pierced
By its own majestic breadth, and fortified
  And pinned it deeper to the soil.   Forlorn
Of thanks be, therefore, no one of these graves !
  Not Hers,[11]—who, at her husband's side, in scorn,
Outfaced the whistling shot and hissing waves,
  Until she felt her little babe unborn
Recoil, within her, from the violent staves
  And bloodhounds of the world,—at which, her life

Dropt inwards from her eyes and followed it
  Beyond the hunters. Garibaldi's wife
And child died so. And now, the seaweeds fit
  Her body, like a proper shroud and coif,
And murmurously the ebbing waters grit
  The little pebbles while she lies interred
In the sea-sand. Perhaps, ere dying thus,
  She looked up in his face (which never stirred
From its clenched anguish) as to make excuse
  For leaving him for his, if so she erred.
He well remembers that she could not choose.

  A memorable grave ! Another is
At Genoa. There, a king [12] may fitly lie,
  Who, bursting that heroic heart of his
At lost Novara, that he could not die,
  (Though thrice into the cannon's eyes for this
He plunged his shuddering steed, and felt the sky
  Reel back between the fire-shocks) stripped away
The ancestral ermine ere the smoke had cleared,
  And, naked to the soul, that none might say
His kingship covered what was base and bleared
  With treason, went out straight an exile, yea,
An exiled patriot. Let him be revered.

  Yea, verily, Charles Albert has died well ;
And if he lived not all so, as one spoke,
  The sin pass softly with the passing-bell :
For he was shriven, I think, in cannon-smoke,
  And, taking off his crown, made visible
A hero's forehead. Shaking Austria's yoke
  He shattered his own hand and heart ' So best,'
His last words were upon his lonely bed,

' I do not end like popes and dukes at least—
Thank God for it.'   And now that he is dead
   Admitting it is proved and manifest
That he was worthy, with a discrowned head,
   To measure heights with patriots, let them stand
Beside the man in his Oporto shroud,
   And each vouchsafe to take him by the hand,
And kiss him on the cheek, and say aloud,—
   ' Thou, too, hast suffered for our native land !
My brother, thou art one of us ! be proud.'

   Still, graves, when Italy is talked upon.
Still, still, the patriot's tomb, the stranger's hate.
   Still Niobe ! still fainting in the sun,
By whose most dazzling arrows violate
   Her beauteous offspring perished ! has she won
Nothing but garlands for the graves, from Fate ?
   Nothing but death-songs ?—Yes, be it understood
Life throbs in noble Piedmont ! while the feet
   Of Rome's clay image, dabbled soft in blood,
Grow flat with dissolution and, as meet,
   Will soon be shovelled off like other mud,
To leave the passage free in church and street.
   And I, who first took hope up in this song,
Because a child was singing one . . . behold,
   The hope and omen were not, haply, wrong !
Poets are soothsayers still, like those of old
   Who studied flights of doves ; and creatures young
And tender, mighty meanings may unfold.

Robert Browning

'DE GUSTIBUS'

I

YOUR ghost will walk, you lover of trees,
　　(If our loves remain)
　　In an English lane,
By a cornfield-side a-flutter with poppies.
Hark, those two in the hazel coppice—
A boy and a girl, if the good fates please,
　　Making love, say,—
　　The happier they!
Draw yourself up from the light of the moon,
And let them pass, as they will too soon,
　　With the bean-flowers' boon,
　　And the blackbird's tune,
　　And May, and June!

II

What I love best in all the world
Is a castle, precipice-encurled,
In a gash of the wind-grieved Apennine.
Or look for me, old fellow of mine,
(If I get my head from out the mouth
O' the grave, and loose my spirit's bands,
And come again to the land of lands)—
In a sea-side house to the farther South,
Where the baked cicala dies of drouth,

And one sharp tree—'tis a cypress—stands,
By the many hundred years red-rusted,
Rough iron-spiked, ripe fruit-o'ercrusted,
My sentinel to guard the sands
To the water's edge.   For, what expands
Before the house, but the great opaque
Blue breadth of sea without a break ?
While, in the house, for ever crumbles
Some fragment of the frescoed walls,
From blisters where a scorpion sprawls.
A girl bare-footed brings, and tumbles
Down on the pavement, green-flesh melons,
And says there 's news to-day—the king
Was shot at, touched in the liver-wing,
Goes with his Bourbon arm in a sling :
—She hopes they have not caught the felons.
Italy, my Italy !
Queen Mary's saying serves for me—
    (When fortune's malice
      Lost her—Calais)—
Open my heart and you will see
Graved inside of it, ' Italy.'
Such lovers old are I and she :
So it always was, so shall ever be !

Arthur Clough

AMOURS DE VOYAGE

[The presence of Arthur Clough in Rome during the brief life of Mazzini's Roman Republic of 1849 has given us this unique piece of literature. I have spoken of it in the Introduction, p. xxiii above. 'Claude's' letters in Canto I. consist of some admirable tourist's remarks and impressions of Rome. In Canto II. he begins to be aware that great modern events are going on among the ruins; that Garibaldi and Mazzini are preparing to defend Rome against the armies of France, who have landed at Civita Vecchia and are marching on Rome to restore the Pope. He witnesses the first repulse of the French on April 30. In Canto III. the course of his half-hearted love affair takes him away to Tuscany, where he resides during the heroic and tragic part of the siege of Rome in June, after the French had returned to the attack in larger force. In Canto v. he hears of the fall of Rome and returns to it, only to leave it again in disgust at the priests and French soldiers now in occupation.]

CANTO I

OVER the great windy waters, and over the clear-crested summits,
Unto the sun and the sky, and unto the perfecter earth,
Come, let us go,—to a land wherein gods of the old time wandered,
Where every breath even now changes to ether divine.
Come, let us go; though withal a voice whisper, 'The world that we live in,
Whithersoever we turn, still is the same narrow crib;

'*Tis but to prove limitation, and measure a cord, that we
travel ;*
  *Let who would 'scape and be free go to his chamber and
  think ;*
'*Tis but to change idle fancies for memories wilfully falser ;*
  '*Tis but to go and have been.'—Come, little bark ! let us go.*

CLAUDE TO EUSTACE

DEAR EUSTATIO, I write that you may write me an
  answer,
Or at the least to put us again *en rapport* with each
  other.
Rome disappoints me much,—St. Peter's, perhaps, in
  especial ;
Only the Arch of Titus and view from the Lateran please
  me :
This, however, perhaps is the weather, which truly is
  horrid.
Greece must be better, surely ; and yet I am feeling so
  spiteful,
That I could travel to Athens, to Delphi, and Troy, and
  Mount Sinai,
Though but to see with my eyes that these are vanity
  also.
  Rome disappoints me much ; I hardly as yet understand,
  but
Rubbishy seems the word that most exactly would suit it.
All the foolish destructions, and all the sillier savings,
All the incongruous things of past incompatible ages,
Seem to be treasured up here to make fools of present and
  future.

Would to Heaven the old Goths had made a cleaner sweep
of it !

Would to Heaven some new ones would come and destroy
these churches !

* * * * * * *

CLAUDE TO EUSTACE

ROME disappoints me still ; but I shrink and adapt myself
to it.

Somehow a tyrannous sense of a superincumbent oppression

Still, wherever I go, accompanies ever, and makes me

Feel like a tree (shall I say ?) buried under a ruin of brickwork.

Rome, believe me, my friend, is like its own Monte
Testaceo,

Merely a marvellous mass of broken and castaway wine-
pots.

Ye gods ! what do I want with this rubbish of ages de-
parted,

Things that Nature abhors, the experiments that she has
failed in ?

What do I find in the Forum ? An archway and two or
three pillars.

Well, but St. Peter's ? Alas, Bernini has filled it with
sculpture !

No one can cavil, I grant, at the size of the great
Coliseum.

Doubtless the notion of grand and capacious and massive
amusement,

This the old Romans had ; but tell me, is this an idea ?

Yet of solidity much, but of splendour little is extant :

'Brickwork I found thee, and marble I left thee!' their
  Emperor vaunted ;
'Marble I thought thee, and brickwork I find thee!' the
  Tourist may answer.

    *   *   *   *   *   *   *

CLAUDE TO EUSTACE

LUTHER, they say, was unwise ; like a half-taught German,
  he could not
See that old follies were passing most tranquilly out of
  remembrance ;
Leo the Tenth was employing all efforts to clear out abuses ;
Jupiter, Juno, and Venus, Fine Arts, and Fine Letters, the
  Poets,
Scholars, and Sculptors, and Painters, were quietly clearing
  away the
Martyrs, and Virgins, and Saints, or at any rate Thomas
  Aquinas :
He must forsooth make a fuss and distend his huge Witten-
  berg lungs, and
Bring back Theology once yet again in a flood upon Europe :
Lo you, for forty days from the windows of heaven it fell ;
  the
Waters prevail on the earth yet more for a hundred and
  fifty ;
Are they abating at last ? the doves that are sent to explore
  are
Wearily fain to return, at the best with a leaflet of pro-
  mise,—
Fain to return, as they went, to the wandering wave-tost
  vessel,—

Fain to re-enter the roof which covers the clean and the
unclean,—

Luther, they say, was unwise ; he didn't see how things
were going ;

Luther was foolish,—but, O great God ! what call you
Ignatius ?

O my tolerant soul, be still ! but you talk of barbarians,

Alaric, Attila, Genseric ;—why, they came, they killed, they

Ravaged, and went on their way ; but these vile, tyrannous
Spaniards,

These are here still,—how long, O ye heavens, in the
country of Dante ?

These, that fanaticized Europe, which now can forget them,
release not

This, their choicest of prey, this Italy ; here you see them,—

Here, with emasculate pupils and gimcrack churches of
Gesu,

Pseudo-learning and lies, confessional-boxes and postures,—

Here, with metallic beliefs and regimental devotions,—

Here, overcrusting with slime, perverting, defacing, de-
basing,

Michael Angelo's Dome, that had hung the Pantheon in
heaven,

Raphael's Joys and Graces, and thy clear stars, Galileo !

   *   *   *   *   *   *   *

GEORGINA TREVELLYN TO LOUISA ——

DEAREST LOUISA,—Inquire, if you please, about Mr.
Claude ——.

He has been once at R., and remembers meeting the H.'s.

Harriet L., perhaps, may be able to tell you about him.

It is an awkward youth, but still with very good manners ;

Not without prospects, we hear ; and, George says, highly
connected.
Georgy declares it absurd, but Mamma is alarmed, and
insists he has
Taken up strange opinions, and may be turning a Papist.
Certainly once he spoke of a daily service he went to.
' Where ? ' we asked, and he laughed and answered, ' At
the Pantheon.'
This was a temple, you know, and now is a Catholic church ;
and
Though it is said that Mazzini has sold it for Protestant
service,
Yet I suppose this change can hardly as yet be effected.
Adieu again,—evermore, my dearest, your loving Georgina.'

    *   *   *   *   *   *   *

Alba,[1] thou findest me still, and, Alba, thou findest me ever,
   Now from the Capitol steps, now over Titus's Arch,
Here from the large grassy spaces that spread from the Lateran
   portal,
   Towering o'er aqueduct lines lost in perspective between,
Or from a Vatican window, or bridge, or the high Coliseum,
   Clear by the garlanded line cut of the Flavian ring.
Beautiful can I not call thee, and yet thou hast power to o'er-
   master,
   Power of mere beauty; in dreams, Alba, thou hauntest me still.
Is it religion ? I ask me ; or is it a vain superstition ?
   Slavery abject and gross ? service, too feeble, of truth ?
Is it an idol I bow to, or is it a god that I worship ?
   Do I sink back on the old, or do I soar from the mean ?
So through the city I wander and question, unsatisfied ever,
   Reverent so I accept, doubtful because I revere.

ARTHUR CLOUGH

CANTO II

Is it illusion? or does there a spirit from perfecter ages,
  Here, even yet, amid loss, change, and corruption abide?
Does there a spirit we know not, though seek, though we find,
    comprehend not,
  Here to entice and confuse, tempt and evade us, abide?
Lives in the exquisite grace of the column disjointed and
    single,
  Haunts the rude masses of brick garlanded gaily with vine,
E'en in the turret fantastic surviving that springs from the
    ruin,
  E'en in the people itself? is it illusion or not?
Is it illusion or not that attracteth the pilgrim transalpine,
  Brings him a dullard and dunce hither to pry and to stare?
Is it illusion or not that allures the barbarian stranger,
  Brings him with gold to the shrine, brings him in arms to
    the gate?

CLAUDE TO EUSTACE

WHAT do the people say, and what does the government
    do?—you
Ask, and I know not at all. Yet fortune will favour your
    hopes; and
I, who avoided it all, am fated, it seems, to describe it.
I, who nor meddle nor make in politics,—I who sincerely
Put not my trust in leagues nor any suffrage by ballot,
Never predicted Parisian millenniums, never beheld a
New Jerusalem coming down dressed like a bride out of
    heaven
Right on the Place de la Concorde,—I, nevertheless, let
    me say it,

Could in my soul of souls, this day, with the Gaul at the
   gates shed
One true tear for thee, thou poor little Roman Republic ;
What, with the German restored, with Sicily safe to the
   Bourbon,
Not leave one poor corner for native Italian exertion ?
France, it is foully done ! and you, poor foolish
   England,—
You, who a twelvemonth ago said nations must choose for
   themselves, you
Could not, of course, interfere,—you, now, when a nation
   has chosen——
Pardon this folly ! The *Times* will, of course, have an-
   nounced the occasion,
Told you the news of to-day ; and although it was slightly
   in error
When it proclaimed as a fact the Apollo was sold to a
   Yankee,
You may believe when it tells you the French are at
   Civita Vecchia.[2]

CLAUDE TO EUSTACE

Dulce it is, and *decorum*, no doubt, for the country to
   fall,—to
Offer one's blood an oblation to Freedom, and die for the
   Cause ; yet
Still, individual culture is also something, and no man
Finds quite distinct the assurance that he of all others is
   called on,
Or would be justified even, in taking away from the world
   that

Precious creature, himself.   Nature sent him here to abide
  here ;
Else why send him at all ?   Nature wants him still, it is
  likely ;
On the whole, we are meant to look after ourselves ; it is
  certain
Each has to eat for himself, digest for himself, and in
  general
Care for his own dear life, and see to his own preservation ;
Nature's intentions, in most things uncertain, in this are
  decisive ;
Which, on the whole, I conjecture the Romans will follow,
  and I shall.
  So we cling to our rocks like limpets ; Ocean may bluster,
Over and under and round us ; we open our shells to im-
  bibe our
Nourishment, close them again, and are safe, fulfilling the
  purpose
Nature intended,—a wise one, of course, and a noble, we
  doubt not.
Sweet it may be and decorous, perhaps, for the country to
  die ; but,
On the whole, we conclude the Romans won't do it, and I
  shan't.

CLAUDE TO EUSTACE

WILL they fight ?   They say so.   And will the French ?
  I can hardly,
Hardly think so ; and yet——He is come, they say, to Palo,
He is passed from Monterone, at Santa Severa
He hath laid up his guns.   But the Virgin, the Daughter of
  Roma,

She hath despised thee and laughed thee to scorn,—The
    Daughter of Tiber,
She hath shaken her head and built barricades against thee !
Will they fight ?   I believe it.   Alas ! 'tis ephemeral folly,
Vain and ephemeral folly, of course, compared with pictures,
Statues, and antique gems !—Indeed : and yet indeed too,
Yet, methought, in broad day did I dream,—tell it not in
    St. James's,
Whisper it not in thy courts, O Christ Church !—yet did I,
    waking,
Dream of a cadence that sings, *Si tombent nos jeunes héros, la
Terre en produit de nouveaux contre vous tous prêts à se battre ;*
Dreamt of great indignations and angers transcendental,
Dreamt of a sword at my side and a battle-horse under-
    neath me.

*　　*　　*　　*　　*　　*　　*

CLAUDE TO EUSTACE

YES, we are fighting at last, it appears.[3]   This morning as
    usual,
Murray, as usual, in hand, I enter the Caffè Nuovo ;
Seating myself with a sense as it were of a change in the
    weather,
Not understanding, however, but thinking mostly of
    Murray,
And, for to-day is their day, of the Campidoglio Marbles ;
Caffè-latte ! I call to the waiter,—and *Non c' è latte,*
This is the answer he makes me, and this is the sign of a
    battle.
So I sit : and truly they seem to think any one else more
Worthy than me of attention.   I wait for my milkless *nero*,

ARTHUR CLOUGH

Free to observe undistracted all sorts and sizes of
  persons,
Blending civilian and soldier in strangest costume, coming
  in, and
Gulping in hottest haste, still standing, their coffee,—with-
  drawing
Eagerly, jangling a sword on the steps, or jogging a
  musket
Slung to the shoulder behind.   They are fewer, moreover,
  than usual,
Much and silenter far ; and so I begin to imagine
Something is really afloat.   Ere I leave, the Caffè is empty,
Empty too the streets, in all its length the Corso
Empty, and empty I see to my right and left the Condotti.
  Twelve o'clock, on the Pincian Hill,[4] with lots of English,
Germans, Americans, French,—the Frenchmen, too, are
  protected,—
So we stand in the sun, but afraid of a probable shower ;
So we stand and stare, and see, to the left of St. Peter's,
Smoke, from the cannon, white,—but that is at intervals
  only,—
Black, from a burning house, we suppose, by the Caval-
  leggieri ;
And we believe we discern some lines of men descending
Down through the vineyard slopes, and catch a bayonet
  gleaming.
Every ten minutes, however,—in this there is no miscon-
  ception,—
Comes a great white puff from behind Michel Angelo's
  dome, and
After a space the report of a real big gun,—not the French-
  man's !—

That must be doing some work.   And so we watch and
    conjecture.
  Shortly, an Englishman comes, who says he has been to
    St. Peter's,
Seen the Piazza and troops, but that is all he can tell us ;
So we watch and sit, and, indeed, it begins to be tire-
    some.—
All this smoke is outside ; when it has come to the inside,
It will be time, perhaps, to descend and retreat to our
    houses.
  Half-past one, or two.   The report of small arms
    frequent,
Sharp and savage indeed ; that cannot all be for nothing :
So we watch and wonder ; but guessing is tiresome, very.
Weary of wondering, watching, and guessing, and gossip-
    ing idly,
Down I go, and pass through the quiet streets with the
    knots of
National Guards patrolling, and flags hanging out at the
    windows,
English, American, Danish,—and, after offering to help an
Irish family moving *en masse* to the Maison Serny,
After endeavouring idly to minister balm to the trembling
Quinquagenarian fears of two lone British spinsters,
Go to make sure of my dinner before the enemy enter.
But by this there are signs of stragglers returning ; and
    voices
Talk, though you don't believe it, of guns and prisoners
    taken ;
And on the walls you read the first bulletin of the
    morning.—
This is all that I saw, and all I know of the battle.

ARTHUR CLOUGH

Claude to Eustace

Victory! Victory!—Yes! ah, yes, thou republican
    Zion,
Truly the kings of the earth are gathered and gone by
    together ;
Doubtless they marvelled to witness such things, were
    astonished, and so forth.
Victory! Victory! Victory!—Ah, but it is, believe
    me,
Easier, easier far, to intone the chant of the martyr
Than to indite any pæan of any victory. Death may
Sometimes be noble ; but life, at the best, will appear an
    illusion.
While the great pain is upon us, it is great ; when it is
    over,
Why, it is over. The smoke of the sacrifice rises to
    heaven,
Of a sweet savour, no doubt, to Somebody ; but on the
    altar,
Lo, there is nothing remaining but ashes and dirt and ill
    odour.
  So it stands, you perceive ; the labial muscles that
    swelled with
Vehement evolution of yesterday Marseillaises,
Articulations sublime of defiance and scorning, to-day col-
Lapse and languidly mumble, while men and women and
    papers
Scream and re-scream to each other the chorus of Victory.
    Well, but
I am thankful they fought, and glad that the Frenchmen
    were beaten.

H   113

CLAUDE TO EUSTACE

So, I have seen a man killed ! An experience that, among
    others !
Yes, I suppose I have ; although I can hardly be certain,
And in a court of justice could never declare I had seen it.
But a man was killed, I am told, in a place where I saw
Something ; a man was killed, I am told, and I saw some-
    thing.
    I was returning home from St. Peter's ; Murray, as
    usual,
Under my arm, I remember ; had crossed the St. Angelo
    bridge ; and
Moving towards the Condotti, had got to the first barricade,
    when
Gradually, thinking still of St. Peter's, I became conscious
Of a sensation of movement opposing me,—tendency this
    way
(Such as one fancies may be in a stream when the wave of
    the tide is
Coming and not yet come,—a sort of noise and retention) ;
So I turned, and, before I turned, caught sight of stragglers
Heading a crowd, it is plain, that is coming behind that
    corner.
Looking up, I see windows filled with heads ; the Piazza,
Into which you remember the Ponte St. Angelo enters,
Since I passed, has thickened with curious groups ; and
    now the
Crowd is coming, has turned, has crossed that last barricade,
    is
Here at my side. In the middle they drag at something.
    What is it ?

Ha ! bare swords in the air, held up ? There seem to be
    voices

Pleading and hands putting back ; official, perhaps ; but
    the swords are

Many, and bare in the air. In the air ? they descend ; they
    are smiting,

Hewing, chopping—At what ? In the air once more up-
    stretched ? And—

Is it blood that 's on them ? Yes, certainly blood ! Of
    whom, then ?

Over whom is the cry of this furor of exultation ?

  While they are skipping and screaming, and dancing
    their caps on the points of

Swords and bayonets, I to the outskirts back, and ask a

Mercantile-seeming bystander, ' What is it ? ' and he,
    looking always

That way, makes me answer, ' A Priest, who was trying to
    fly to

The Neapolitan army,'—and thus explains the proceeding.

  You didn't see the dead man ? No ;—I began to be
    doubtful ;

I was in black myself, and didn't know what mightn't
    happen,—

But a National Guard close by me, outside of the hubbub,

Broke his sword with slashing a broad hat covered with
    dust,—and

Passing away from the place with Murray under my arm,
    and

Stooping, I saw through the legs of the people the legs of
    a body.

  You are the first, do you know, to whom I have men-
    tioned the matter.

Whom should I tell it to else ?—these girls ?—the Heavens
    forbid it !—
Quidnuncs at Monaldini's ?—Idlers upon the Pincian ?
  If I rightly remember, it happened on that afternoon
    when
Word of the nearer approach of a new Neapolitan army
First was spread. I began to bethink me of Paris
    Septembers,
Thought I could fancy the look of that old 'Ninety-two.
    On that evening
Three or four, or, it may be, five, of these people were
    slaughtered.
Some declared they had, one of them, fired on a sentinel ;
    others
Say they were only escaping ; a Priest, it is currently
    stated,
Stabbed a National Guard on the very Piazza Colonna :
History, Rumour of Rumours, I leave to thee to determine !
  But I am thankful to say the government seems to have
    strength to
Put it down ; it has vanished, at least ; the place is most
    peaceful.
Through the Trastevere walking last night, at nine of the
    clock, I
Found no sort of disorder ; I crossed by the Island-
    bridges,
So by the narrow streets to the Ponte Rotto, and
    onwards
Thence by the Temple of Vesta, away to the great
    Coliseum,
Which at the full of the moon is an object worthy
    a visit.

ARTHUR CLOUGH

ONLY think, dearest Louisa, what fearful scenes we have
    witnessed !—

   *   *   *   *   *   *   *

George has just seen Garibaldi, dressed up in a long white
    cloak, on
Horseback, riding by, with his mounted negro behind him :
This is a man, you know, who came from America with
    him,
Out of the woods, I suppose, and uses a *lasso* in fighting,
Which is, I don't quite know, but a sort of noose, I imagine ;
This he throws on the heads of the enemy's men in a battle,
Pulls them into his reach, and then most cruelly kills them :
Mary does not believe, but we heard it from an Italian.
Mary allows she was wrong about Mr. Claude *being selfish* ;
He was *most* useful and kind on the terrible thirtieth of April.
Do not write here any more ; we are starting directly for
    Florence :
We should be off to-morrow, if only Papa could get horses ;
All have been seized everywhere for the use of this dreadful
    Mazzini.

   *   *   *   *   *   *   *

CLAUDE TO EUSTACE

IT is most curious to see what a power a few calm words (in
Merely a brief proclamation) appear to possess on the
    people.
Order is perfect, and peace ; the city is utterly tranquil ;
And one cannot conceive that this easy and *nonchalant*
    crowd, that

Flows like a quiet stream through street and market-place, entering
Shady recesses and bays of church, *osteria*, and *caffè*,
Could in a moment be changed to a flood as of molten lava,
Boil into deadly wrath and wild homicidal delusion.

Ah, 'tis an excellent race,—and even in old degradation,
Under a rule that enforces to flattery, lying, and cheating,
E'en under Pope and Priest, a nice and natural people.
Oh, could they but be allowed this chance of redemption !—but clearly
That is not likely to be. Meantime, notwithstanding all journals,
Honour for once to the tongue and the pen of the eloquent writer !
Honour to speech ! and all honour to thee, thou noble Mazzini !

* * * * * * *

CANTO III

CLAUDE TO EUSTACE

FAREWELL, Politics, utterly ! What can I do ? I cannot
Fight, you know ; and to talk I am wholly ashamed. And although I
Gnash my teeth when I look in your French or your English papers,
What is the good of that ? Will swearing, I wonder, mend matters ?
Cursing and scolding repel the assailants ? No, it is idle ;
No, whatever befalls, I will hide, will ignore or forget it.
Let the tail shift for itself ; I will bury my head. And what 's the

Roman Republic to me, or I to the Roman Republic ?
  Why not fight ?—In the first place, I haven't so much as
    a musket ;
In the next, if I had, I shouldn't know how I should
    use it ;
In the third, just at present I 'm studying ancient marbles ;
In the fourth, I consider I owe my life to my country ;
In the fifth—I forget, but four good reasons are ample.
Meantime, pray let 'em fight, and be killed.   I delight in
    devotion.
So that I 'list not, hurrah for the glorious army of martyrs !
Sanguis martyrum semen Ecclesiæ ; though it would seem
    this
Church is indeed of the purely Invisible, Kingdom-come
    kind :
Militant here on earth !   Triumphant, of course, then, else-
    where !
Ah, good Heaven, but I would I were out far away from
    the pother !

*   *   *   *   *   *   *

CLAUDE TO EUSTACE

TIBUR is beautiful, too, and the orchard slopes, and the
    Anio
Falling, falling yet, to the ancient lyrical cadence ;
Tibur and Anio's tide ; and cool from Lucretilis ever,
With the Digentian stream, and with the Bandusian foun-
    tain,
Folded in Sabine recesses, the valley and villa of Horace :—
So not seeing I sang ; so seeing and listening say I,
Here as I sit by the stream, as I gaze at the cell of the Sibyl,

Here with Albunea's home and the grove of Tiburnus
    beside me ; *
Tivoli beautiful is, and musical, O Teverone,
Dashing from mountain to plain, thy parted impetuous
    waters,
Tivoli's waters and rocks ; and fair unto Monte Gennaro
(Haunt, even yet, I must think, as I wander and gaze, of the
    shadows,
Faded and pale, yet immortal, of Faunus, the Nymphs, and
    the Graces),
Fair in itself, and yet fairer with human completing
    creations,
Folded in Sabine recesses the valley and villa of Horace :—
So not seeing I sang ; so now—Nor seeing, nor hearing,
Neither by waterfall lulled, nor folded in sylvan embraces,
Neither by cell of the Sibyl, nor stepping the Monte Gennaro,
Seated on Anio's bank, nor sipping Bandusian waters,
But on Montorio's height, looking down on the tile-clad
    streets, the
Cupolas, crosses, and domes, the bushes and kitchen-gardens,
Which, by the grace of the Tiber, proclaim themselves
    Rome of the Romans,—
But on Montorio's height, looking forth to the vapoury
    mountains,
Cheating the prisoner Hope with illusions of vision and
    fancy,—
But on Montorio's height, with these weary soldiers by me,
Waiting till Oudinot enter, to reinstate Pope and Tourist.

    *   *   *   *   *   *   *

---

*   —— domus Albuneæ resonantis,
    Et præceps Anio, et Tiburni lucus, et uda
    Mobilibus pomaria rivis.

ARTHUR CLOUGH

CANTO V

CLAUDE TO EUSTACE,—*from Florence*

ROME is fallen, I hear, the gallant Medici taken,
Noble Manara slain, and Garibaldi has lost *il Moro* ; ⁵—
Rome is fallen ; and fallen, or falling, heroical Venice.
I, meanwhile, for the loss of a single small chit of a
    girl, sit
Moping and mourning here,—for her, and myself much
    smaller.
  Whither depart the souls of the brave that die in the
    battle,
Die in the lost, lost fight, for the cause that perishes with
    them ?
Are they upborne from the field on the slumberous pinions
    of angels
Unto a far-off home, where the weary rest from their
    labour,
And the deep wounds are healed, and the bitter and burning
    moisture
Wiped from the generous eyes ? or do they linger, unhappy,
Pining, and haunting the grave of their bygone hope and
    endeavour ?
  All declamation, alas ! though I talk, I care not for Rome
    nor
Italy ; feebly and faintly, and but with the lips, can
    lament the
Wreck of the Lombard youth, and the victory of the
    oppressor.
Whither depart the brave ?—God knows ; I certainly do
    not.

CLAUDE TO EUSTACE,—*from Rome*

ROME will not suit me, Eustace; the priests and soldiers
    possess it;
Priests and soldiers :—and, ah! which is the worst, the
    priest or the soldier?
  Politics, farewell, however! For what could I do?
    with inquiring,
Talking, collating the journals, go fever my brain about
    things o'er
Which I can have no control. No, happen whatever may
    happen,
Time, I suppose, will subsist; the earth will revolve on
    its axis;
People will travel; the stranger will wander as now in the
    city;
Rome will be here, and the Pope the *custode* of Vatican
    marbles.

      *   *   *   *   *   *   *

So go forth to the world, to the good report and the evil!
  Go, little book! thy tale, is it not evil and good?
Go, and if strangers revile, pass quietly by without answer.
 Go, and if curious friends ask of thy rearing and age,
Say, 'I am flitting about many years from brain unto brain of
  Feeble and restless youths born to inglorious days :
But,' so finish the word, 'I was writ in a Roman chamber,
  When from Janiculan heights thundered the cannon of
  France.'

Arthur Clough

PESCHIERA

[This poem and its sequel 'Alteram Partem' were extorted from Clough on his return journey from Rome in 1849, by his grief at seeing the Lombard plain reoccupied by the Austrians after the suppression of the gallant and repeated struggles of North Italy. Peschiera, one of the four fortresses of the Venetian 'Quadrilateral,' had been in the centre of the struggle, and its fall had marked the turn of the tide. Brescia, the most patriotic of all the cities of Italy, had defended itself gallantly and suffered atrocious cruelties at the hands of General Haynau.]

WHAT voice did on my spirit fall,
Peschiera, when thy bridge I crost ?
' 'Tis better to have fought and lost,
Than never to have fought at all.'

The tricolour—a trampled rag
Lies, dirt and dust ; the lines I track
By sentry boxes yellow-black,
Lead up to no Italian flag.

I see the Croat soldier stand
Upon the grass of your redoubts ;
The eagle with his black wings flouts
The breath and beauty of your land.

Yet not in vain, although in vain,
O men of Brescia, on the day
Of loss past hope, I heard you say
Your welcome to the noble pain.

You say, ' Since so it is,—good-bye
Sweet life, high hope ; but whatsoe'er
May be, or must, no tongue shall dare
To tell, " The Lombard feared to die ! " '

You said (there shall be answer fit),
' And if our children must obey,
They must ; but thinking on this day
'Twill less debase them to submit.'

You said (Oh not in vain you said),
' Haste, brothers, haste, while yet we may ;
The hours ebb fast of this one day
When blood may yet be nobly shed.'

Ah ! not for idle hatred, not
For honour, fame, nor self-applause,
But for the glory of the cause,
You did, what will not be forgot.

And though the stranger stand, 'tis true,
By force and fortune's right he stands ;
By fortune, which is in God's hands,
And strength, which yet shall spring in you.

This voice did on my spirit fall,
Peschiera, when thy bridge I crost,
' 'Tis better to have fought and lost,
Than never to have fought at all.'

ARTHUR CLOUGH

ALTERAM PARTEM

OR shall I say, Vain word, false thought,
　　Since Prudence hath her martyrs too,
And Wisdom dictates not to do,
Till doing shall be not for nought ?

Not ours to give or lose is life ;
Will Nature, when her brave ones fall,
Remake her work ? or songs recall
Death's victim slain in useless strife ?

That rivers flow into the sea
Is loss and waste, the foolish say,
Nor know that back they find their way,
Unseen, to where they wont to be.

Showers fall upon the hills, springs flow,
The river runneth still at hand,
Brave men are born into the land,
And whence the foolish do not know.

No ! no vain voice did on me fall,
Peschiera, when thy bridge I crost,
' *'Tis* better to have fought and lost,
Than never to have fought at all.'

Mrs. Hamilton King

UGO BASSI

[Mrs. Hamilton King's religious epic on 'Ugo Bassi,' in the *Disciples*, is historically faithful as a portrait of Ugo Bassi, and as a representation of the Christian side of the Italian movement of 1848-49. This short extract presents a scene in the last stages of Garibaldi's retreat from Rome to the Adriatic in the late summer of 1849, after the siege described in Clough's *Amours de Voyage*. Garibaldi and the remnants of his army, surrounded on all sides by Austrians, is trying to escape down to Cesenatico on the Adriatic coast. He has with him his wife Anita, the friar saint Ugo Bassi (the subject of the poem), and Ciceruacchio the Roman demagogue—all three doomed to perish in a few days. The ultimate triumph of the survivor, Garibaldi, which the poetess makes Ugo prophesy, took place in 1860.]

FORWARD we went all day in gloom and dread
    For Garibaldi's eyes had grown so dark,
And his mouth set so stern, I did not dare
To look upon him ; and I felt the days
Were drawing to some terrible great close.

    *   *   *   *   *   *

    And that night in the open we encamped,
To the sea-coast advancing.   It was dark ;
More than one fire we did not dare to light ;
And near it Garibaldi and his wife,
And Ciceruacchio and his two sons sat,
With Ugo and some others, through the night.

    *   *   *   *   *   *

MRS. HAMILTON KING

The wakeful eyes
Of Garibaldi strained into the dark ;
And still he listened, and would take no rest.
And by the watchfire that night once he broke
The gloomy silence, saying : ' Friend, good-night !
What shall to-morrow bring us ?   Shall we reach
Venice together ?   Nay, I think it not.
For we have come to our last hope, and that
Is failing us, to die amongst our own.
What matters ?   What is left us now to do,
Since this year's Italy was but a dream,
And it is over, but to vanish too ?
We could not save her,—should we save ourselves ?
Nay, it were well for us if but our blood
Might drop into her furrows, and sink down,
And through the winter lie among the seeds,
And we be no more heard of evermore :
For I know surely that though we be dead,
Though all this generation pass away,
Out of this soil the flower shall spring at last,
Of the starry whiteness, and the crimson heart,
And the green leaves spreading—Yea, the Flower of
    the World,
Poets have dreamed of—but upon our graves.'

And Ugo answered, with the flickering fire
Lighting the liquid eyes up underneath :
' Yea, Greatest, on our graves, but not on thine.
Thine eyes shall see it.   They have got no look
Of yearning after a dream unfulfilled ;
But rather that magnetic joy which draws
Men to partake of it, saying, " We desire,

And falter, and come short ; lo, here is one
In whom the strength is one with the desire."
Though now thou comest to that straitest pass
Wherein availeth thee not strength, nor joy,
And thou must suffer, and not thou alone.
But thou shalt come forth from it, though thou leave
Thy heart's desire there, and thy bloom of life,
And God shall go with thee through the dark days
That are coming, that are come.   And thou shalt stand,
Some day far hence, after long tale of years,
Alone, alone, but Garibaldi still,
In the face of all the world ; and at thy side,
Like a golden lily after the night's rain
Bursting its sheath in the sunrise, all uprisen,
Italy, Italy, with the eyes of fire !
Laying her hand in thine, and turned to thee,
And saying, " My Saviour ! can I give thee nought ? "
And then thy heart will turn back to this day,
This day of utter desolate despair,
When we were driven between the shore and sea,
And the hounds of all the Empire loose on us,—
And yet we were together ; and the heart
Of thy child's mother lying close to thine :
And thou wilt say in the glory to thyself,
" Give me that day back—but it cannot be."
Yet fear not, Garibaldi, for thy heart
Is stronger than all grief, or death, or time.'

Swinburne

TO AURELIO SAFFI

[This poem, written after the death of Mazzini in 1872, recalls the time, many years before, when Swinburne first met Saffi at Oxford. Saffi, the intimate friend of Mazzini, had been co-Triumvir with Mazzini and Armellini during the defence of Rome in 1849, described in Clough's poem above. It is those events of 1849 to which verses II, III, and IV of this poem refer. Verses V, VI, and VII refer to the time at which the poem was written, after 1872, when Italy has been united, but Mazzini 'who spake and it was done' is dead. Swinburne attributes the union of Italy to the original inspiration of Mazzini rather than to the wit of the 'wise man' Cavour, or the hand of the 'strong man' Garibaldi.]

I

YEAR after year has fallen on sleep, till change
    Hath seen the fourth part of a century fade,
Since you, a guest to whom the vales were strange
    Where Isis whispers to the murmuring shade
    Above her face by winds and willows made,
And I, elate at heart with reverence, met.
Change must give place to death ere I forget
The pride that change of years has quenched not yet.

II

Pride from profoundest humbleness of heart
    Born, self-uplift at once and self-subdued,
Glowed, seeing his face whose hand had borne such part,
    In so sublime and strange vicissitude

As then filled all faint hearts with hope renewed
To think upon and triumph ; though the time
Were dense and foul with darkness cast from crime
Across the heights that hope was fain to climb.

III

Hope that had risen, a sun to match the sun
   That fills and feeds all Italy with light,
Had set, and left the crowning work undone
   That raised up Rome out of the shadow of night :
   Yet so to have won the worst, to have fought the fight,
Seemed, as above the grave of hope cast down
Stood faith, and smiled against the whole world's frown,
A conquest lordlier than the conqueror's crown.

IV

To have won the worst that chance could give, and worn
   The wreath of adverse fortune as a sign
More bright than binds the brows of victory, borne
   Higher than all trophies borne of tyrants shine—
   What lordlier gift than this, what more divine,
Can earth or heaven make manifest, and bid
Men's hearts bow down and honour ?   Fate lies hid,
But not the work that true men dared and did.

V

The years have given and taken away since then
   More than was then foreseen of hope or fear.
Fallen are the towers of empire : all the men
   Whose names made faint the heart of the earth to hear

Are broken as the trust they held so dear
Who put their trust in princes : and the sun
Sees Italy, as he in heaven is, one ;
But sees not him who spake, and this was done.

VI

Not by the wise man's wit, the strong man's hand,
　By swordsman's or by statesman's craft or might,
Sprang life again where life had left the land,
　And light where hope nor memory now saw light :
　Not first nor most by grace of these was night
Cast out, and darkness driven before the day
Far as a battle-broken host's array
Flies, and no force that fain would stay it can stay.

VII

One spirit alone, one soul more strong than fate,
　One heart whose heat was as the sundawn's fire,
Fed first with flame as heaven's immaculate
　Faith, worn and wan and desperate of desire :
　And men that felt that sacred breath suspire
Felt by mere speech and presence fugitive
The holy spirit of man made perfect give
Breath to the lips of death, that death might live.

　　*　　　*　　　*　　　*　　　*　　　*　　　*

Walter Savage Landor

EPIGRAM. [ON THE FRENCH]

[In 1849 the reactionary and clerical French Republicans had brought the Pope back, over the corpses of the Garibaldini on the Janiculum, to resume his rule in Rome. In 1851 the French Republic perished by the *coup d'état* of Louis Napoleon, following in the steps of his uncle the great Emperor.]

O WRETCHED despicable slaves,
    Accomplices and dupes of knaves!
The cut-throat uncle laid ye low,
The cut-purse nephew gags ye now.
Behold at last the vengeance come
For the brave men ye slew at Rome.

Swinburne

A WATCH IN THE NIGHT

[This poem applies to such a period of reaction as followed the suppression of the '48.]

I

WATCHMAN, what of the night ?—
    Storm and thunder and rain,
Lights that waver and wane,
Leaving the watchfires unlit.
Only the balefires are bright,
    And the flash of the lamps now and then
From a palace where spoilers sit,
    Trampling the children of men.

II

Prophet, what of the night ?—
    I stand by the verge of the sea,
    Banished, uncomforted, free,
Hearing the noise of the waves
And sudden flashes that smite
    Some man's tyrannous head,
Thundering, heard among graves
    That hide the hosts of his dead.

III

Mourners, what of the night ?—
   All night through without sleep
   We weep, and we weep, and we weep.
Who shall give us our sons ?
Beaks of raven and kite,
   Mouths of wolf and of hound,
Give us them back whom the guns
   Shot for you dead on the ground.

IV

Dead men, what of the night ?—
   Cannon and scaffold and sword,
   Horror of gibbet and cord,
Mowed us as sheaves for the grave,
Mowed us down for the right.
   We do not grudge or repent.
Freely to freedom we gave
   Pledges, till life should be spent.

V

Statesman, what of the night ?—
   The night will last me my time.
   The gold on a crown or a crime
Looks well enough yet by the lamps.
Have we not fingers to write,
   Lips to swear at a need ?
Then, when danger decamps,
   Bury the word with the deed.[1]

VI

Warrior, what of the night ?—
  Whether it be not or be
  Night, is as one thing to me.
I for one, at the least,
Ask not of dews if they blight,
  Ask not of flames if they slay,
Ask not of prince or of priest
  How long ere we put them away.

VII

Master, what of the night ?—
  Child, night is not at all
  Anywhere, fallen or to fall,
Save in our star-stricken eyes.
Forth of our eyes it takes flight,
  Look we but once nor before
Nor behind us, but straight on the skies ;
  Night is not then any more.

VIII

Exile, what of the night ?—
  The tides and the hours run out,
  The seasons of death and of doubt,
The night-watches bitter and sore.
In the quicksands leftward and right
  My feet sink down under me ;
But I know the scents of the shore
  And the broad blown breaths of the sea.

IX

Captives, what of the night ?—
　　It rains outside overhead
　　Always, a rain that is red,
And our faces are soiled with the rain.
Here in the seasons' despite
　　Day-time and night-time are one,
Till the curse of the kings and the chain
　　Break, and their toils be undone.

X

Christian, what of the night ?—
　　I cannot tell ; I am blind.
　　I halt and hearken behind
If haply the hours will go back
And return to the dear dead light,
　　To the watchfires and stars that of old
Shone where the sky now is black,
　　Glowed where the earth now is cold.

XI

High priest, what of the night ?—
　　The night is horrible here
　　With haggard faces and fear,
Blood, and the burning of fire.[2]
Mine eyes are emptied of sight,
　　Mine hands are full of the dust.
If the God of my faith be a liar,
　　Who is it that I shall trust ?

XII

Princes, what of the night ?—
Night with pestilent breath
Feeds us, children of death,
Clothes us close with her gloom.
Rapine and famine and fright
　　Crouch at our feet and are fed.
Earth where we pass is a tomb,
　　Life where we triumph is dead.

XIII

Martyrs, what of the night ?—
　　Nay, is it night with you yet ?
　　We, for our part, we forget
What night was, if it were.
The loud red mouths of the fight
　　Are silent and shut where we are.
In our eyes the tempestuous air
　　Shines as the face of a star.

XIV

England, what of the night ?—
　　Night is for slumber and sleep,
　　Warm, no season to weep.
Let me alone till the day.
Sleep would I still if I might,
　　Who have slept for two hundred years.
Once I had honour, they say ;
　　But slumber is sweeter than tears.

XV

France, what of the night ?—
 Night is the prostitute's noon,
 Kissed and drugged till she swoon,
Spat upon, trod upon, whored.
With bloodred rose-garlands dight,
 Round me reels in the dance
Death, my saviour, my lord,
 Crowned ; there is no more France.[3]

XVI

Italy, what of the night ?—
 Ah, child, child, it is long !
 Moonbeam and starbeam and song
Leave it dumb now and dark.
Yet I perceive on the height
 Eastward, not now very far,
A song too loud for the lark,
 A light too strong for a star.

XVII

Germany, what of the night ?—
 Long has it lulled me with dreams ;
 Now at midwatch, as it seems,
Light is brought back to mine eyes,
And the mastery of old and the might
 Lives in the joints of mine hands,
Steadies my limbs as they rise,
 Strengthens my foot as it stands.

SWINBURNE

XVIII

Europe, what of the night ?—
   Ask of heaven, and the sea,
   And my babes on the bosom of me,
Nations of mine, but ungrown.
There is one who shall surely requite
   All that endure or that err :
She can answer alone :
   Ask not of me, but of her.

XIX

Liberty, what of the night ?—
   I feel not the red rains fall,
   Hear not the tempest at all,
Nor thunder in heaven any more.
All the distance is white
   With the soundless feet of the sun.
Night, with the woes that it wore,
   Night is over and done.

Swinburne

A SONG IN TIME OF ORDER. 1852

[The same theme as *A Watch in the Night*, treated in a different mood.   Three Republican exiles are escaping from Europe.]

PUSH hard across the sand,
    For the salt wind gathers breath ;
Shoulder and wrist and hand,
    Push hard as the push of death.

The wind is as iron that rings,
    The foam-heads loosen and flee ;
It swells and welters and swings,
    The pulse of the tide of the sea.

And up on the yellow cliff
    The long corn flickers and shakes ;
Push, for the wind holds stiff,
    And the gunwale dips and rakes.

Good hap to the fresh fierce weather,
    The quiver and beat of the sea !
While three men hold together,
    The kingdoms are less by three.

SWINBURNE

Out to the sea with her there,
  Out with her over the sand ;
Let the kings keep the earth for their share !
  We have done with the sharers of land.

They have tied the world in a tether,
  They have bought over God with a fee ;
While three men hold together,
  The kingdoms are less by three.

We have done with the kisses that sting,
  The thief's mouth red from the feast,
The blood on the hands of the king
  And the lie at the lips of the priest.

Will they tie the winds in a tether,
  Put a bit in the jaws of the sea ?
While three men hold together,
  The kingdoms are less by three.

Let our flag run out straight in the wind !
  The old red shall be floated again
When the ranks that are thin shall be thinned,
  When the names that were twenty are ten ;

When the devil's riddle is mastered
  And the galley-bench creaks with a Pope,
We shall see Buonaparte the bastard
  Kick heels with his throat in a rope.

While the shepherd sets wolves on his sheep
 And the emperor halters his kine,
While Shame is a watchman asleep
 And Faith is a keeper of swine,

Let the wind shake our flag like a feather,
 Like the plumes of the foam of the sea !
While three men hold together,
 The kingdoms are less by three.

All the world has its burdens to bear,
 From Cayenne to the Austrian whips ;
Forth, with the rain in our hair
 And the salt sweet foam in our lips :

In the teeth of the hard glad weather,
 In the blown wet face of the sea ;
While three men hold together,
 The kingdoms are less by three.

Elizabeth Barrett Browning

THE FORCED RECRUIT

SOLFERINO, 1859

[In 1859 Napoleon III. brought the power of France to aid King Victor Emmanuel of Piedmont to drive the Austrians out of North Italy. At the battles of Magenta and Solferino the Austrians were driven for ever out of Lombardy, though not yet out of Venice. This story explains itself: the Austrians enforced the conscription in Italy as elsewhere in their polyglot empire.]

I

IN the ranks of the Austrian you found him,
    He died with his face to you all ;
Yet bury him here where around him
    You honour your bravest that fall.

II

Venetian, fair-featured and slender,
    He lies shot to death in his youth,
With a smile on his lips over-tender
    For any mere soldier's dead mouth.

III

No stranger, and yet not a traitor,
    Though alien the cloth on his breast,
Underneath it how seldom a greater
    Young heart, has a shot sent to rest !

143

IV

By your enemy tortured and goaded
  To march with them, stand in their file,
His musket (see) never was loaded,
  He facing your guns with that smile !

V

As orphans yearn on to their mothers,
  He yearned to your patriot bands ;—
' Let me die for our Italy, brothers,
  If not in your ranks, by your hands !

VI

' Aim straightly, fire steadily ! spare me
  A ball in the body which may
Deliver my heart here, and tear me
  This badge of the Austrian away ! '

VII

So thought he, so died he this morning,
  What then ? many others have died.
Ay, but easy for men to die scorning
  The death-stroke, who fought side by side—

VIII

One tricolour floating above them ;
  Struck down 'mid triumphant acclaims
Of an Italy rescued to love them
  And blazon the brass with their names.

ELIZABETH BARRETT BROWNING

IX

But he,—without witness or honour,
  Mixed, shamed in his country's regard,
With the tyrants who march in upon her,
  Died faithful and passive : 'twas hard.

X

'Twas sublime.   In a cruel restriction
  Cut off from the guerdon of sons,
With most filial obedience, conviction,
  His soul kissed the lips of her guns.

XI

That moves you ?   Nay, grudge not to show it,
  While digging a grave for him here :
The others who died, says your poet,
  Have glory,—let *him* have a tear.

Elizabeth Barrett Browning

A COURT LADY

[An incident in hospital during the Lombard campaign of 1859 illustrating the union of various provinces of Italy in the one cause, and also the French alliance. The Romagnole, the Lombard, and the Tuscan were freed by this campaign of the armies of France and Piedmont, but the Venetian not.]

I

HER hair was tawny with gold, her eyes with purple
    were dark,
Her cheeks' pale opal burnt with a red and restless spark.

II

Never was lady of Milan nobler in name and in race :
Never was lady of Italy fairer to see in the face.

III

Never was lady on earth more true as woman and wife,
Larger in judgment and instinct, prouder in manners and
    life.

IV

She stood in the early morning, and said to her maidens,
    ' Bring
That silken robe made ready to wear at the court of the
    king.

V

' Bring me the clasps of diamond, lucid, clear of the mote,
Clasp me the large at the waist, and clasp me the small at
    the throat.

VI

' Diamonds to fasten the hair, and diamonds to fasten the
    sleeves,
Laces to drop from their rays like a powder of snow from
    the eaves.'

VII

Gorgeous she entered the sunlight which gathered her up
    in a flame,
While, straight in her open carriage, she to the hospital
    came.

VIII

In she went at the door, and gazing from end to end,
' Many and low are the pallets, but each is the place of a
    friend.'

IX

Up she passed through the wards, and stood at a young
    man's bed :
Bloody the band on his brow, and livid the droop of his
    head.

X

' Art thou a Lombard, my brother ? Happy art thou,'
    she cried,
And smiled like Italy on him : he dreamed in her face and
    died.

XI

Pale with his passing soul, she went on still to a second :
He was a grave hard man, whose years by dungeons were
reckoned.

XII

Wounds in his body were sore, wounds in his life were sorer.
' Art thou a Romagnole ? ' Her eyes drove lightnings
before her.

XIII

' Austrian and priest had joined to double and tighten the
cord
Able to bind thee, O strong one,—free by the stroke of a
sword.

XIV

' Now be grave for the rest of us, using the life overcast
To ripen our wine of the present (too new) in glooms of the
past.'

XV

Down she stepped to a pallet where lay a face like a girl's,
Young, and pathetic with dying,—a deep black hole in the
curls.

XVI

' Art thou from Tuscany, brother ? and seest thou, dreaming in pain,
Thy mother stand in the piazza, searching the List of the
slain ? '

ELIZABETH BARRETT BROWNING

XVII

Kind as a mother herself, she touched his cheeks with her
    hands :
' Blessed is she who has borne thee, although she should
    weep as she stands.'

XVIII

On she passed to a Frenchman, his arm carried off by a
    ball :
Kneeling, . . . ' O more than my brother ! how shall I
    thank thee for all ?

XIX

' Each of the heroes around us has fought for his land and
    line,
But *thou* hast fought for a stranger, in hate of a wrong not
    thine.

XX

' Happy are all free peoples, too strong to be dispossessed.
But blessed are those among nations, who dare to be strong
    for the rest ! '

XXI

Ever she passed on her way, and came to a couch where
    pined
One with a face from Venetia, white with a hope out of
    mind.

XXII

Long she stood and gazed, and twice she tried at the name,
But two great crystal tears were all that faltered and came.

XXIII

Only a tear for Venice ?—she turned as in passion and loss,
And stooped to his forehead and kissed it, as if she were
    kissing the cross.

XXIV

Faint with that strain of heart she moved on then to
    another,
Stern and strong in his death. ' And dost thou suffer, my
    brother ? '

XXV

Holding his hands in hers :—' Out of the Piedmont lion
Cometh the sweetness of freedom ; sweetest to live or to
    die on.'

XXVI

Holding his cold rough hands,—' Well, oh, well have ye
    done
In noble, noble Piedmont, who would not be noble alone.'

XXVII

Back he fell while she spoke. She rose to her feet with a
    spring,—
' That was a Piedmontese ! and this is the Court of the
    King.'

Elizabeth Barrett Browning

NAPOLEON III. IN ITALY

[For a brief explanation of the complicated issues raised in this poem see Introduction, p. xxvii, above. It is in praise of Napoleon III. for coming to liberate Italy from Austria in the campaign of 1859, the 'deed' to which Stanzas V. to the end refer. The first four stanzas refer to the establishment of Napoleon's empire in France, which can be viewed either as a criminally acquired despotism or as a popularly chosen dictatorship, according as we emphasise its origin in the *coup d'état* of December 1851, or the confirmation of the results of the *coup d'état* by nearly 'eight millions' of votes in the plebiscite of November 1852, referred to by Mrs. Browning in Stanza I.]

I

EMPEROR, Emperor!
    From the centre to the shore,
From the Seine back to the Rhine,
Stood eight millions up and swore
By their manhood's right divine
    So to elect and legislate,
This man should renew the line
Broken in a strain of fate
And leagued kings at Waterloo,
When the people's hands let go.
    Emperor
    Evermore.

II

With a universal shout
They took the old regalia out
From an open grave that day;
From a grave that would not close,
Where the first Napoleon lay
   Expectant, in repose,
As still as Merlin, with his conquering face
Turned up in its unquenchable appeal
To men and heroes of the advancing race,—
   Prepared to set the seal
Of what has been on what shall be.
    Emperor
    Evermore.

III

The thinkers stood aside
To let the nation act.[1]
Some hated the new-constituted fact
Of empire, as pride treading on their pride.
Some quailed, lest what was poisonous in the past
Should graft itself in that Druidic bough
   On this green now.
  Some cursed, because at last
The open heavens to which they had look'd in vain
For many a golden fall of marvellous rain
   Were closed in brass; and some
Wept on because a gone thing could not come;
And some were silent, doubting all things for
   That popular conviction,—evermore
   Emperor.

152

IV

That day I did not hate
Nor doubt, nor quail nor curse.
I, reverencing the people, did not bate
My reverence of their dead and oracle,
 Nor vainly prate
 Of better and of worse
Against the great conclusion of their will.
 And yet, O voice and verse,
Which God set in me to acclaim and sing
Conviction, exaltation, aspiration,
We gave no music to the patent thing,
Nor spared a holy rhythm to throb and swim
 About the name of him
Translated to the sphere of domination
 By democratic passion !
 I was not used, at least,
 Nor can be, now or then,
 To stroke the ermine beast
 On any kind of throne
(Though builded by a nation for its own),
And swell the surging choir for kings of men—
 ' Emperor
 Evermore.'

V

 But now, Napoleon, now
That, leaving far behind the purple throng
 Of vulgar monarchs, thou
 Tread'st higher in thy deed
 Than stair of throne can lead,

To help in the hour of wrong
The broken hearts of nations to be strong,—
   Now, lifted as thou art
   To the level of pure song,
We stand to meet thee on these Alpine snows !
And while the palpitating peaks break out
Ecstatic from somnambular repose
With answers to the presence and the shout,
We, poets of the people, who take part
With elemental justice, natural right,
   Join in our echoes also, nor refrain.
We meet thee, O Napoleon, at this height
At last, and find thee great enough to praise.
Receive the poet's chrism, which smells beyond
   The priest's, and pass thy ways ;—
An English poet warns thee to maintain
God's word, not England's :—let His truth be true
And all men liars ! with His truth respond
To all men's lie.   Exalt the sword and smite
On that long anvil of the Apennine
Where Austria forged the Italian chain in view
Of seven consenting nations, sparks of fine
   Admonitory light,
Till men's eyes wink before convictions new.
Flash in God's justice to the world's amaze,
Sublime Deliverer !—after many days
Found worthy of the deed thou art come to do—
   Emperor
   Evermore.

VI

But Italy, my Italy,
Can it last, this gleam ?
Can she live and be strong,
Or is it another dream
Like the rest we have dreamed so long ?
  And shall it, must it be,
That after the battle-cloud has broken
She will die off again
Like the rain,
Or like a poet's song
Sung of her, sad at the end
Because her name is Italy,—
Die and count no friend ?
Is it true,—may it be spoken,—
That she who has lain so still,
With a wound in her breast,
And a flower in her hand,
And a grave-stone under her head,
While every nation at will
Beside her has dared to stand
And flout her with pity and scorn,
Saying, ' She is at rest,
She is fair, she is dead,
And, leaving room in her stead
To Us who are later born,
This is certainly best ! '
Saying, ' Alas, she is fair,
Very fair, but dead,
And so we have room for the race.'
—Can it be true, be true,
That she lives anew ?

That she rises up at the shout of her sons,
At the trumpet of France,
And lives anew ?—is it true
That she has not moved in a trance,
As in Forty-eight ?
When her eyes were troubled with blood
Till she knew not friend from foe,
Till her hand was caught in a strait
Of her cerement and baffled so
From doing the deed she would ;
And her weak foot stumbled across
The grave of a king,
And down she dropt at heavy loss,
And we gloomily covered her face and said,
' We have dreamed the thing ;
She is not alive, but dead.'

VII

Now, shall we say
Our Italy lives indeed ?
And if it were not for the beat and bray
Of drum and trump of martial men,
Should we feel the underground heave and strain,
Where heroes left their dust as a seed
   Sure to emerge one day ?
And if it were not for the rhythmic march
Of France and Piedmont's double hosts,
   Should we hear the ghosts
Thrill through ruined aisle and arch,
Throb along the frescoed wall,
Whisper an oath by that divine
They left in picture, book, and stone,

That Italy is not dead at all ?
Ay, if it were not for the tears in our eyes,
These tears of a sudden passionate joy,
   Should we see her arise
From the place where the wicked are overthrown,
   Italy, Italy ? loosed at length
   From the tyrant's thrall,
Pale and calm in her strength ?
Pale as the silver cross of Savoy
When the hand that bears the flag is brave,
And not a breath is stirring, save
   What is blown
Over the war-trump's lip of brass,
Ere Garibaldi forces the pass ! [2]

VIII

Ay, it is so, even so.
Ay, and it shall be so.
Each broken stone that long ago
She flung behind her as she went
In discouragement and bewilderment
Through the cairns of Time, and missed her way
   Between to-day and yesterday,
   Up springs a living man.
And each man stands with his face in the light
   Of his own drawn sword,
Ready to do what a hero can.
Wall to sap, or river to ford,
Cannon to front, or foe to pursue,
Still ready to do, and sworn to be true,
   As a man and a patriot can.
Piedmontese, Neapolitan,

Lombard, Tuscan, Romagnole,[3]
Each man's body having a soul,—
Count how many they stand,
All of them sons of the land.
Every live man there
Allied to a dead man below,
And the deadest with blood to spare
To quicken a living hand
In case it should ever be slow.
Count how many they come
To the beat of Piedmont's drum,
With faces keener and grayer
Than swords of the Austrian slayer,
All set against the foe.
    ' Emperor
    Evermore.'

IX

Out of the dust, where they ground them,
Out of the holes, where they dogged them,
Out of the hulks, where they wound them
In iron, tortured and flogged them ;
Out of the streets, where they chased them,
Taxed them and then bayonetted them,—
Out of the homes, where they spied on them
(Using their daughters and wives),
Out of the church, where they fretted them,
Rotted their souls and debased them,
Trained them to answer with knives,
Then cursed them all at their prayers !—
Out of cold lands, not theirs,
Where they exiled them, starved them, lied on them ;

Back they come like a wind, in vain
Cramped up in the hills, that roars its road
The stronger into the open plain ;
Or like a fire that burns the hotter
And longer for the crust of cinder,
Serving better the ends of the potter ;
Or like a restrainèd word of God,
Fulfilling itself by what seems to hinder.
   ' Emperor
   Evermore.'

x

Shout for France and Savoy !
Shout for the helper and doer.
Shout for the good sword's ring,
Shout for the thought still truer.
Shout for the spirits at large
Who passed for the dead this spring,
Whose living glory is sure.
Shout for France and Savoy !
Shout for the council and charge !
Shout for the head of Cavour ;
And shout for the heart of a King
That 's great with a nation's joy.
   Shout for France and Savoy !

XI

Take up the child, Macmahon,[4] though
Thy hand be red
From Magenta's dead,
And riding on, in front of the troop,
  In the dust of the whirlwind of war

159

Through the gate of the city of Milan, stoop
And take up the child to thy saddle-bow,
Nor fear the touch as soft as a flower
   Of his smile as clear as a star !
Thou hast a right to the child, we say,
Since the women are weeping for joy as those
Who, by thy help and from this day,
   Shall be happy mothers indeed.
They are raining flowers from terrace and roof :
   Take up the flower in the child.
While the shout goes up of a nation freed
   And heroically self-reconciled,
Till the snow on that peaked Alp aloof
Starts, as feeling God's finger anew,
And all those cold white marble fires
Of mounting saints on the Duomo-spires
   Flicker against the Blue.
     ' Emperor
     Evermore.'

XII

   Ay, it is He,[5]
Who rides at the King's right hand !
Leave room to his horse and draw to the side,
Nor press too near in the ecstasy
Of a newly delivered impassioned land :
    He is moved, you see,
    He who has done it all.
They call it a cold stern face ;
   But this is Italy
Who rises up to her place !—

For this he fought in his youth,
Of this he dreamed in the past;
The lines of the resolute mouth
Tremble a little at last.
Cry, he has done it all!
    'Emperor
    Evermore.'

XIII

It is not strange that he did it,
Though the deed may seem to strain
To the wonderful, unpermitted,
For such as lead and reign.
But he is strange, this man:
The people's instinct found him
(A wind in the dark that ran
Through a chink where was no door),
And elected him and crowned him
    · Emperor
    Evermore.

XIV

Autocrat? let them scoff,
    Who fail to comprehend
That a ruler incarnate of
    The people, must transcend
All common king-born kings.
These subterranean springs
A sudden outlet winning,
Have special virtues to spend.
The people's blood runs through him,

Dilates from head to foot,
Creates him absolute,
And from this great beginning
Evokes a greater end
To justify and renew him—
    Emperor
    Evermore.

*   *   *   *   *   *

XIX

Great is he,
Who uses his greatness for all.
His name shall stand perpetually
    As a name to applaud and cherish,
Not only within the civic wall
For the loyal, but also without
    For the generous and free.
    Just is he,
Who is just for the popular due
    As well as the private debt.
The praise of nations ready to perish
    Fall on him,—crown him in view
    Of tyrants caught in the net,
And statesmen dizzy with fear and doubt !
And though, because they are many,
    And he is merely one,
And nations selfish and cruel
Heap up the inquisitor's fuel
To kill the body of high intents,
And burn great deeds from their place,
Till this, the greatest of any
May seem imperfectly done ;

ELIZABETH BARRETT BROWNING

III

Peace, peace, peace, do you say ?
    What !—uncontested, undenied ?
    Because we triumph, we succumb ?
A pair of Emperors stand in the way,
    (One of whom is a man, beside)
    To sign and seal our cannons dumb ?

IV

No, not Napoleon !—he who mused
    At Paris, and at Milan spake,
    And at Solferino led the fight :
Not he we trusted, honoured, used
    Our hopes and hearts for . . . till they break—
    Even so, you tell us . . . in his sight.

V

Peace, peace, is still your word ?
    We say you lie then !—that is plain.
    There *is* no peace, and shall be none.
Our very Dead would cry 'Absurd ! '
    And clamour that they died in vain,
    And whine to come back to the sun.

VI

Hush ! more reverence for the Dead !
    They 've done the most for Italy
    Evermore since the earth was fair.
Now would that *we* had died instead,
    Still dreaming peace meant liberty,
    And did not, could not mean despair.

VII

Peace, you say ?—yes, peace, in truth !
    But such a peace as the ear can achieve
    'Twixt the rifle's click and the rush of the ball,
'Twixt the tiger's spring and the crunch of the tooth,
    'Twixt the dying atheist's negative
    And God's Face—waiting, after all !

Elizabeth Barrett Browning

AN AUGUST VOICE

[Here Mrs. Browning goes back to the movement of Tuscan liberation, the failure of which she had witnessed in 1849 from *Casa Guidi Windows*. In 1859, during the Lombard campaign, Tuscany, together with Parma, Modena, and Romagna, had risen and driven out their Grand Dukes and other tyrants. By the Treaty of Villafranca, referred to in the poem above, these tyrants were to be restored; but the States of Central Italy, led by Tuscany's 'iron baron' Ricasoli, refused to take back their old governments, and continued for ten months to demand annexation to Victor Emmanuel's kingdom. In this they were finally successful, being supported not only by North Italy but by England: also Napoleon could not, and would not, compel them by force of arms to submit again to tyrannies from which his own action had in fact just released them. Mrs. Browning, who always saw Napoleon on his best side, here puts into his mouth an imaginary oration, in which he ironically exhorts the Tuscans to 'take back their Grand Duke,'—on the principle of ' don't nail his ears to the pump.' The 'Grand Duke' is the Duke Leopold of *Casa Guidi Windows*, who had in 1848 sworn to a constitution, and then broken his word and brought back Radetzky's Austrians.]

I

YOU 'LL take back your Grand Duke?
   I made the treaty upon it.
Just venture a quiet rebuke;
   Dall' Ongaro write him a sonnet;
Ricasoli gently explain
   Some need of the constitution:
He 'll swear to it over again,
   Providing an 'easy solution.'
You 'll call back the Grand Duke.

167

II

You 'll take back your Grand Duke ?
  I promised the Emperor Francis
To argue the case by his book,
  And ask you to meet his advances.
The Ducal cause, we know
  (Whether you or he be the wronger)
Has very strong points ;—although
  Your bayonets, there, have stronger.
You 'll call back the Grand Duke.

III

You 'll take back your Grand Duke ?
  He is not pure altogether.
For instance, the oath which he took
  (In the Forty-eight rough weather)
He 'd ' nail your flag to his mast,'
  Then softly scuttled the boat you
Hoped to escape in at last,
  And both by a ' Proprio motu.'
You 'll call back the Grand Duke.

IV

You 'll take back your Grand Duke ?
  The scheme meets nothing to shock it
In this smart letter, look,
  We found in Radetsky's pocket ;
Where his Highness in sprightly style
  Of the flower of his Tuscans wrote,
' These heads be the hottest in file ;
  Pray shoot them the quickest.'   Quote,
And call back the Grand Duke.

III

' Good,' said the King as he passed.
  Was he cold to the arts ?—or else coy
To possession ? or crossed, at the last,
  (Whispered some) by the vote in Savoy ? [1]
  Shout ! Love him enough for his joy !
' Good,' said the King as he passed.

IV

He, travelling the whole day through flowers
  And protesting amenities, found
At Pistoia, betwixt the two showers
  Of red roses, the ' Orphans ' (renowned
  As the heirs of Puccini) who wound
With a sword through the crowd and the flowers.

V

' 'Tis the sword of Castruccio,[2] O King,—
  In that strife of intestinal hate,
Very famous ! Accept what we bring,
  We who cannot be sons, by our fate,
  Rendered citizens by thee of late,
And endowed with a country and king.

VI

' Read ! Puccini has willed that this sword
  (Which once made in an ignorant feud
Many orphans) remain in our ward
  Till some patriot its pure civic blood
  Wipe away in the foe's and make good,
In delivering the land by the sword.'

VII

Then the King exclaimed, ' This is for *me* ! '
  And he dashed out his hand on the hilt,
While his blue eye shot fire openly,
  And his heart overboiled till it spilt
  A hot prayer,—' God ! the rest as Thou wilt !
But grant me this !—*This* is for *me*.'

VIII

O Victor Emanuel, the King,
  The sword is for *thee*, and the deed,
And nought for the alien, next spring,
  Nought for Hapsburg and Bourbon agreed—
  But, for us, a great Italy freed,
With a hero to head us,—our King !

VII

' Yet through Varese's cannon-smoke
   My eye saw clear : men feared this man
   At Como, where this sword could seal
Death's protocol with every stroke : [3]
   And now . . . the drop there scarcely can
   Impair the keenness of the steel.

VIII

' So man and sword may have their use ;
   And if the soil beneath my foot
   In valour's act is forfeited,
I 'll strike the harder, take my dues
   Out nobler, and all loss confute
   From ampler heavens above my head.

IX

' My King, King Victor, I am thine !
   So much Nice-dust as what I am
   (To make our Italy) must cleave.
Forgive that.'   Forward with a sign
   He went.
            You 've seen the telegram ?
Palermo 's taken, we believe.

Swinburne

A SONG IN TIME OF REVOLUTION. 1860

[Referring to the liberation of South and Central Italy in 1860, when Garibaldi and his volunteers liberated Sicily and Naples from the Bourbon, and Victor Emmanuel's regular army liberated Umbria and the Marches from the Pope.]

THE heart of the rulers is sick, and the high-priest covers
    his head :
For this is the song of the quick that is heard in the ears
    of the dead.

The poor and the halt and the blind are keen and mighty
    and fleet :
Like the noise of the blowing of wind is the sound of the
    noise of their feet.

The wind has the sound of a laugh in the clamour of days
    and of deeds :
The priests are scattered like chaff, and the rulers broken
    like reeds.

The high-priest sick from qualms, with his raiment bloodily
    dashed ;
The thief with branded palms, and the liar with cheeks
    abashed.